WINDOWS SERVER 2022 ADMINISTRATION SIMPLIFIED

A SIMPLE STEP BY STEP GUIDE

By

Dr Bienvenue Maula

Contents

INTRODUCTION

Windows Server is a line of **Microsoft operating systems** (OSes) comprised of extremely powerful machines. Windows Server was first launched in April 2003. It's typically installed on heavy-use servers serving as a backbone for most IT companies, applications, and services. The server handles the administrative group-related activities on a network. It organizes, stores, sends, and receives files from devices connected to a network.

A server is a computer in your network that provides services and resources to other devices such as computers .

A client requests services and resources from the server.

A service can be :

1. Folders
2. E-mails
3. Movies
4. Etc,...

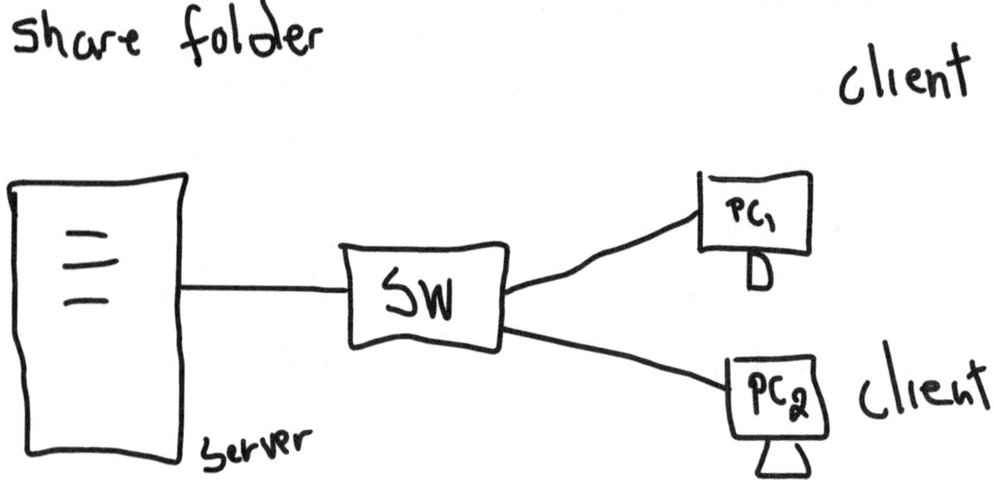

A **resource** can be :

1.hard disk drives

2. printers

3.cameras

4.etc,...

PC1 and **PC2** will have to store folders in a centralized server.

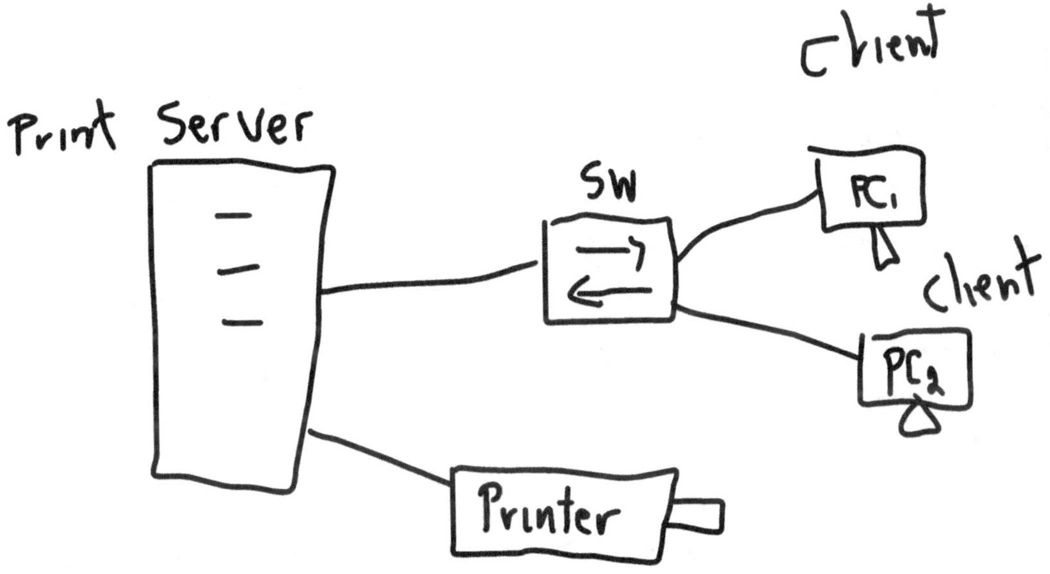

For printing, **PC1** and **PC2** will have to wait the permission of the server.

A **server** is a computer program or equipment that offers a service to another computer program and its users, referred to collectively as the clients. **The physical system** that a server program runs on is sometimes referred to as a server in a data center. That machine may be a dedicated server, or it could be utilized for anything else. In a client/server programming architecture, a server program waits for requests from client programs, which **could be running on the same machine or on a different** one. One program on a computer can act as both a client and a server when other programs ask for its services.

The services provided by a server include three primary categories of service:

Network Services

Network services include any service that exists to provide network functionality. For example, the Dynamic Host Confi guration Protocol (DHCP) is used to provide Internet Protocol (IP) confi guration settings that allow client devices to communicate on the network. Another example is the Domain Name System (DNS) server service, which resolves Internet-like domain names to IP addresses. These Internet-like names are called hostnames.

Security Services

Security services include those services that provide authentication, authorization,

confidentiality, or some form of protection to the network and networked devices. An example of a security service is the Active Directory Domain Service (AD DS), which could also be partially categorized as a network service. AD DS provides the user accounts that are used to log on to Windows Server-based networks. When these accounts are used for logon processes, authentication is performed and authentication is a security service. An additional security service is the IPSec Policy Service, which enforces security settings for Internet Protocol (IP)-based communications.

1	Authentication ⟶	Username/passowrd	Make sure everybody must login
2	Authorization ⟶	Write/Read Permission	Give access according to job description
3	Accounting ⟶	Logs/event,….	Monitor how users are accessing the system

Information Services

Information services include any service that provides information access, information management, or information processing.

For example, the Microsoft SQL Server service provides database access and database management. This functionality qualifi es SQL Server as an information service. Microsoft SharePoint is another example of an information service. It provides for information storage and retrieval, as well as collaboration.

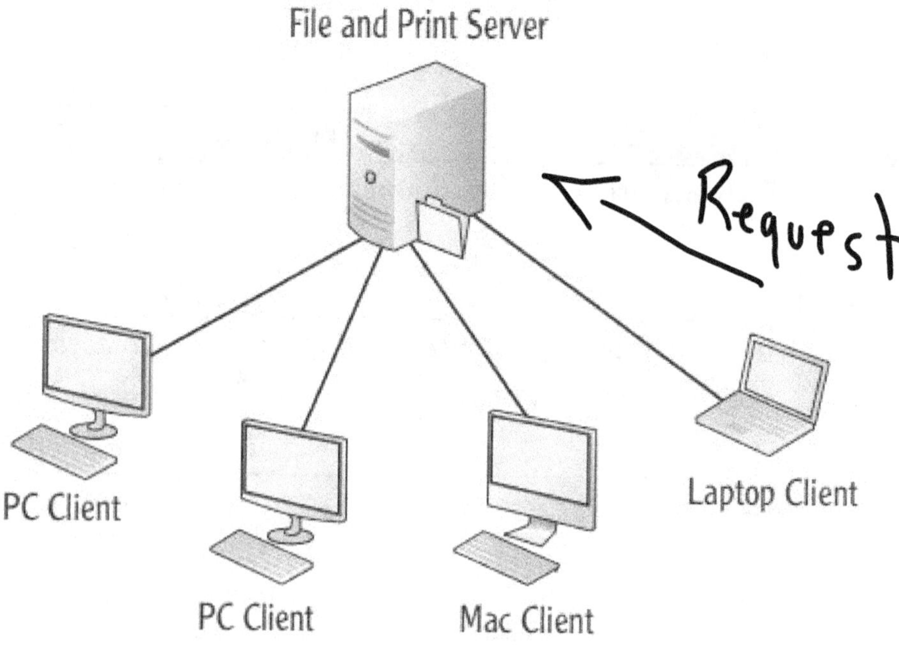

Typical Server Characteristics	Typical Client Characteristics
Used by many users	Used by one user at a time
Built from high-quality components	Built from average quality components
Optimized for background applications	Optimized for visual foreground applications
Provides services to the network	Consumes services from the network

Windows Server versions

When it comes to networking, Windows Server has become the standard. For the last 16 years, Microsoft has released a major version of Windows Server every four years and a minor version every two years. The minor versions can be recognized with the suffix R2. The Windows operating system is persistently updated to add new functionality to match the needs of today's users. Administrators need to understand how their server has evolved and upgraded. The list of all major and minor Microsoft Windows Server versions is as follows:

- **Windows Server 2000:** Microsoft dropped the NT version from its system to emphasize new Windows capabilities. This edition included networking features, such as XMP support and the ability to create active server pages. This edition also created specialized versions for server environments with the help of its Advanced Server and a Datacenter edition.

- **Windows Server 2003:** This was the first version of Windows developed by Microsoft as a part of its NT family of operating systems. The release of Windows Server 2003 brought a significant difference. The objective of Windows Server 2003 was to reduce the need to reboot the system. It provided the ability to install updates without restarting the system. Another feature of

Windows Server 2003 was its ability to define server roles, which enabled IT teams to customize operating systems for specific tasks like DNS servers. Windows Server 2003 came with multiple versions, including the Standard, Advanced, and Datacenter versions.

o **Windows Server 2008:** This server edition was the third release of the Windows Server operating system. It brought on the Windows Server operating system, which included improvements to Active Directory (AD) and changes in the OS software support features and network services. One of the significant enhancements observed was the Microsoft Hyper-V system. This enabled users to create virtual machines (VMs) to give an advantage to Windows users in the competitive market. This version also included new administration tools known as Event Viewer and Server Manager to provide more control to administrators over important server activities.

o **Windows Server 2008 R2:** Windows Server 2008 R2 was an updated 2008 edition in 2009. The significant changes found in this version were due to the transition from Windows Vista to being based on Windows 7. This change not only brought the system to a 64-bit environment but included other technical updates on supporting services. This version brought additional updates to AD, better group policy implementation, and new services. It also provided better server access to users in remote locations with DirectAccess and BranchCache.

- **Windows Server 2012:** This version is the fifth edition of the Windows Server operating system. Unlike its predecessor, this version has four editions (Foundation, Essentials, Standard, and Datacenter) with various improved features, such as an IP address management role, an updated version of Hyper-V, an all-new Windows Task Manager, updated versions of PowerShell and Server Core, and a new file system known as ReFS. Microsoft added new functionalities to Windows Server 2012 and marketed the new version as Cloud OS to become more competitive in the cloud. The improved functionality enabled users to employ the Hyper-V architecture easily with other new cloud technologies. The changes made to support this included updates to the storage system, the addition of the Hyper-V Virtual Switch , and the inclusion of Hyper-V Replica.

- **Windows Server 2012 R2:** Windows Server 2012 R2 was an updated version of Windows 2012. It was released in 2013 with many changes and improvements to Windows 12 functionalities so it could integrate with cloud services. One of these changes included rewrites to both network services and security protocols. Updates also included the introduction of

PowerShell and Desired State Configuration systems designed to enhance the network configuration management. Another update improved the functionality of storage systems, provided better and easier access for file sharing, and enhanced distributed file replication.

- **Windows Server 2016:** Windows Server 2016 is the seventh edition of the Windows Server operating system. It was the successor to the Windows 8-based Windows Server 2012 and was developed concurrently with Windows 10. This version introduced a new server, Nano Server. This server was a scaled-down version with a limited interface designed to make it secure. This release also introduced Network Controller, which administrators could use to help them manage physical and virtual network devices from a single location. This release also enhanced the VM system to support the use of containers, make their interaction with Docker easier, and support encryption for Hyper-V. Windows Server 2016 came with two editions: Standard and Datacenter.

- **Windows Server 2019:** Windows Server 2019 is the most used Windows Server version. It was released in October 2018 and included comprehensive features to meet emerging networking requirements, including the following:

    1. **Windows Admin Center:** The Windows Admin Center was designed

to centralize server management. It also includes several tools IT teams can use daily for things such as configuration management, performance monitoring, and managing services running on different servers.

2. **Hyper Converged Infrastructure (HCI):** Microsoft moved to virtualization after adding Hyper-V in Windows Server 2008. VMs in the latest Windows version included enhanced HCI features built to give network administrators the ability to manage virtualized services.

3. **Microsoft Defender Advanced Threat Protection:** One of the major concerns of businesses today is cybersecurity, particularly advanced persistent threats. Attackers use whaling, spear phishing, and social media profiling to gain entry to the network, and antivirus systems can help prevent these attacks. This provides advanced threat protection against emerging cyberattacks. Microsoft released Microsoft Defender ATP as part of Windows Server 2019. It not only monitors accounts for suspicious activity but tracks the activities of users, prevents unauthorized changes, and

- automatically investigates attacks. It also provides options for remediation
  - **Windows Server 2022** introduces advanced multi-layer security, hybrid capabilities with Azure, and a flexible application platform. As part of this release, we are bringing secured-core capabilities to help protect hardware, firmware, and Windows Server OS capabilities against advanced security threats. Secured-core server builds on technologies such as Windows Defender System Guard and Virtualization-based Security to minimize risk from firmware vulnerabilities and advanced malware. The new release also provides secured connectivity that introduces several new capabilities such as faster and more secure encrypted HTTPS connections, industry standard SMB AES 256 encryption and more.
  - Windows Server 2022 improves hybrid server management with significantly improved VM management, an enhanced event viewer, and many more new capabilities in Windows Admin Center. Furthermore, this release includes significant improvements to Windows containers, such as smaller image sizes for faster download, simplified network policy implementation and containerization tools for .NET applications.

CHAPTER 1: Downloading and Installing Microsoft Windows Server 2022

As a **Windows Server administrator**, you must keep the infrastructure secure, available, and flexible. If you prefer to install the 10th and latest LTSC release of the Windows Server OS, join us with the Complete Guide to Install Microsoft Windows Server 2022. Three years after Windows Server 2019, Microsoft released Windows Server 2022 on August 18.

Windows Server 2022 is the operating system that large organizations trust. However, if you are managing small-to-medium-sized businesses, follow the steps of this tutorial to start working with Windows Server 2022. In the end, you will be able to enjoy the new and more efficient features of Windows Server 2022 to increase your system performance.

Why You Should Choose Windows Server 2022?

Previously, you reviewed Windows Server 2019 Installation. Built on the solid basis of Windows Server 2019, Windows Server 2022 introduces numerous advances in the areas of security, Azure hybrid integration and administration, and application platform. Advanced multi-layer security, hybrid capabilities with Azure, and a configurable application platform are all features of Windows Server 2022. We are introducing secured-core capabilities as part of this version to aid in safeguarding hardware, firmware, and Windows Server OS capabilities against cutting-edge security threats.

A secured-core server reduces the risk of firmware flaws and sophisticated malware by relying on technologies like Windows Defender System Guard and Virtualization-based Security. AES 256 encryption for SMB, which is the industry standard, and faster and more secure encrypted HTTPS connections are just a few of the new features included in the new release's secured connectivity.

Customers may continue to run their workloads securely, create new hybrid cloud scenarios, and upgrade existing applications with Windows Server 2022 to satisfy changing business requirements. When you decide to Install Windows Server 2022, you better be aware of its editions which are: Essentials, Standard, Datacenter, and Azure Datacenter.

Main Reasons to Install Microsoft Windows Server 2022

With the new technical capabilities that come with Windows Server 2022, you can modernize your server environment. Let's know more here. Also if you are thinking of **Upgrading to Windows Server 2022**, the below explanations might be efficient.

- **Advanced multi-layered security**: Windows Server has always placed a strong emphasis on security. You may benefit from multi-layer security in this release thanks to Secured-core server and Secured connectivity. With the Secured-core server's cutting-edge defense across hardware, firmware, and virtualization layers, IT and SecOps teams are able to implement complete security extensively throughout their environment.

- **Flexible application platform**: When you install Windows Server 2022 or even upgrade to this version, you can benefit from scalability enhancements like support for 48TB of memory and 2,048 logical cores running on 64 physical sockets for those demanding Tier1 applications. Also, it is possible to benefit from improvements to Windows containers in this release. Windows Server 2022, for instance, increases the interoperability of

Windows containers with third-party applications, adds HostProcess containers for node setup, supports IPv6 and dual-stack, and makes it possible to execute network policies consistently with Calico. Additionally, we're still working with the Kubernetes community to add container support for Windows Server 2022 and add the additional features to both the Azure Kubernetes Service (AKS) and AKS on Azure Stack HCI.

- **Hybrid capabilities with Azure**: To digitally modernize your businesses, you can choose a hybrid or multi-cloud solution. By connecting to Azure Arc, you may now use on-premises Windows Server 2022 to benefit from cloud services. Additionally, you can benefit from File Server improvements like SMB Compression in Windows Server 2022. By compressing data as it travels over a network, SMB Compression enhances application file transfer. Last but not least, the beloved among admins Windows Admin Center tool offers a contemporary server management experience with features like a new event viewer and gateway proxy support for Azure-linked scenarios.

Prerequisites to Install Windows Server 2022

To let this tutorial works correctly, provide the Windows Server 2022 minimum hardware and system requirements.

- **Server**: _Buying a Dedicated Server_ to prepare for Installation.
- **CPU**: 1.4 GHz x86-64 processor.
- **RAM**: 2 GB.
- **Disk space**: At least 32 GB free space.
- **Network**: A wireless adapter that supports 802.11, an Ethernet adapter capable of at least 1 gigabit per second throughput, or a NIC card with a minimum bandwidth of 1 Gbit/s.
- **Graphics**: 1024 x 768 pixels display
- **BIOS**: UEFI 2.3.1c-based system and firmware that supports secure boot (only required for certain features)
- **Choosing Installation Option.**

Windows Server 2022 Installation Option; Which one to Choose?

Customers who download the entire ISO will have to pick an installation method and an edition. The Datacenter and Standard editions are the subject of this ISO review. The most comprehensive edition is the Datacenter edition, which also offers unlimited server virtualization in addition to the additional Datacenter-specific features.

Installation Options:

1. **Server Core**: The installation method that **is advised** is this one. It is a more compact installation that supports all server roles and has the essential parts of Windows Server but lacks a local graphical user interface (GUI). It is employed for "headless" deployments that are controlled from a distance using the Windows Admin Center, PowerShell, or other server administration programs.
2. **Server with Desktop Experience**: For customers (Especially organizations) who prefer this alternative, this is a complete installation and includes a full GUI.

However, it is up to you to choose which option best suits your needs and preferences. Do your choice and move on.

CHAPTER 2: Install Windows Server 2022 [Step by Step with Screenshots]

Let's go through the steps of the Windows Server 2022 installation tutorial. It helps you take your job more seriously and keep your data secure. Windows Server 2022 is designed for professionals. Install Microsoft Windows 2022 and be one of them!

Step 1. Prepare to Install & Download the Windows Server 2022 ISO

Obtaining the installation file is the first and most important step in installing the new version of Windows Server 2022. This file is an ISO that has exactly the same information as an optical disc. You can use this file to make a bootable disk on which to install your new server operating system. You must first register on Microsoft's official Windows Insider page in order to get the Windows Server 2022 ISO image. You can use any browser to access this website.

Then, from the menu that appears, choose **Download the ISO** by clicking on Windows Server 2022. Then click **Next**.

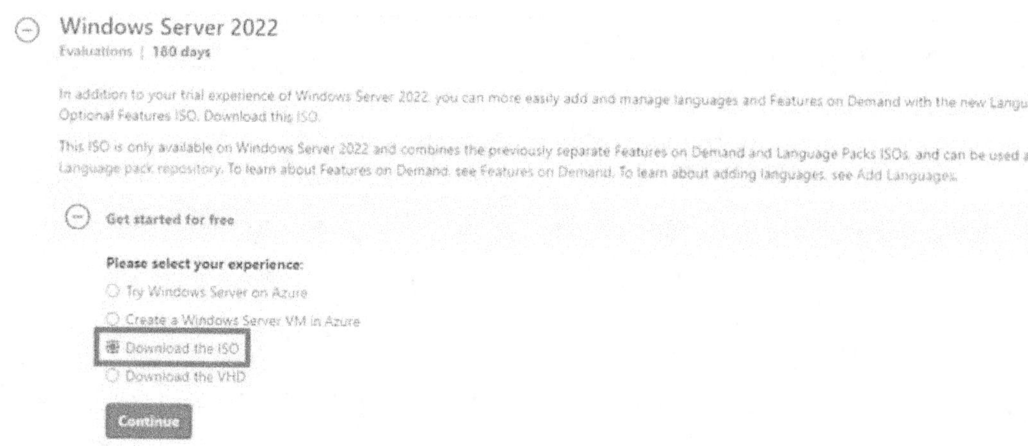

To be eligible for downloading the _Windows Server 2022 ISO file_, you must fill out your details. Make sure you accurately enter your information. Click "**Continue**" when finished.

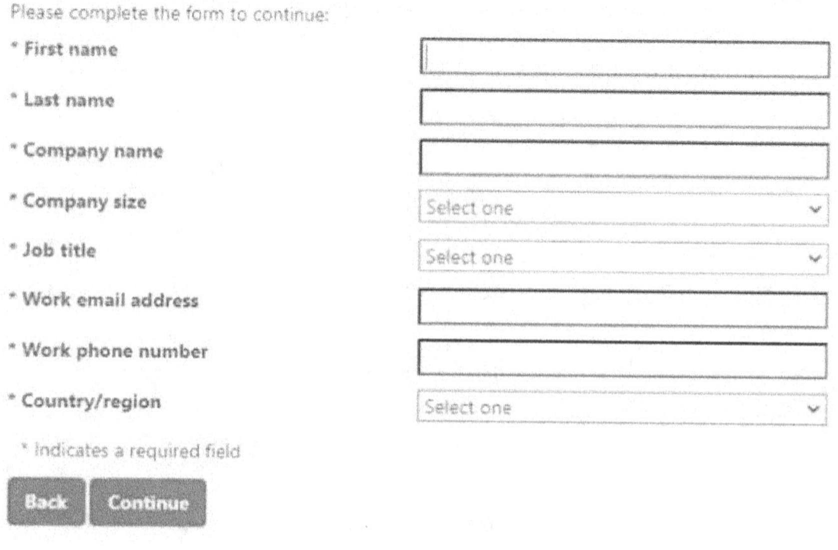

When installing Windows Server 2022, select the language you want to use. There are now 8 languages available. After choosing, press the **Download** button.

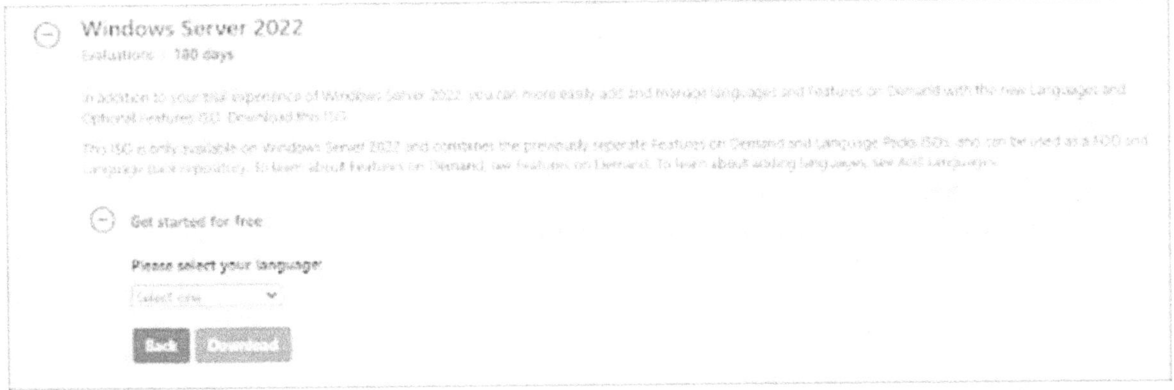

It can take the download several hours to finish. Wait till the end.

Step 2. Install Microsoft Windows Server 2022

Power on your physical or virtual machine. It is time to get on with the installation process. Once the below screen is displayed, select your preferred language, keyboard layout preference, and time/currency settings. When you are finished, click "**Next**" and continue.

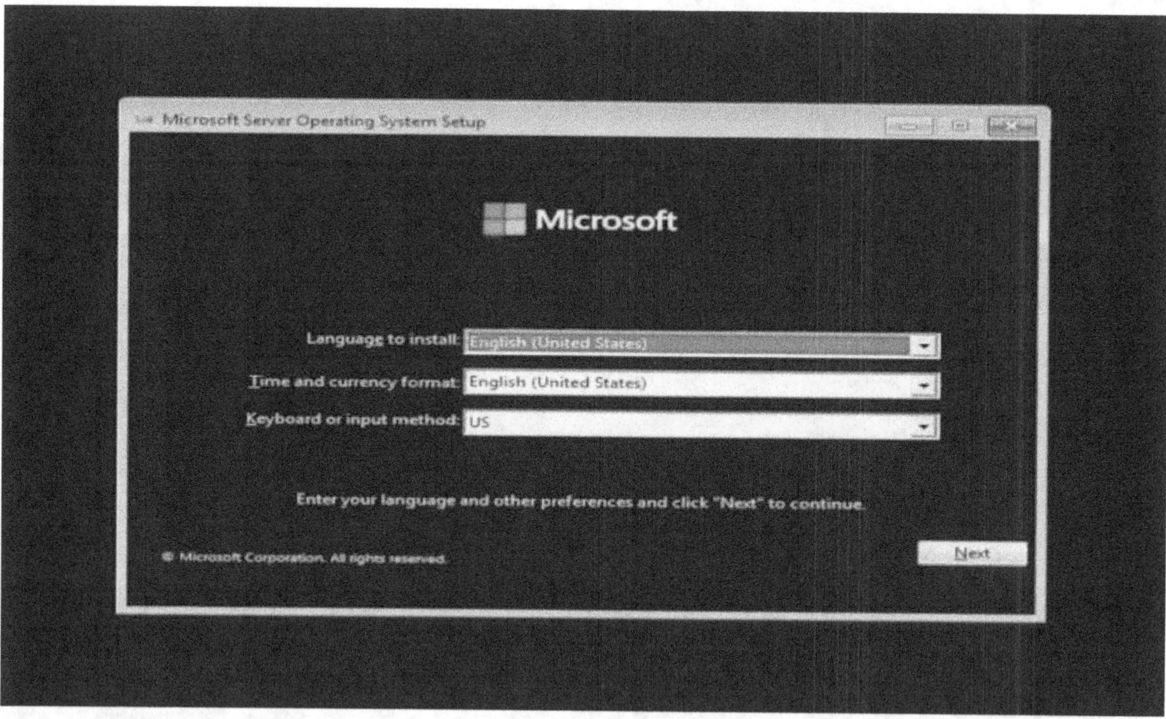

To start the Windows Server 2022 installation procedure, click the **Install Now** option. The Server Core edition of Microsoft's server platform will now start to install.

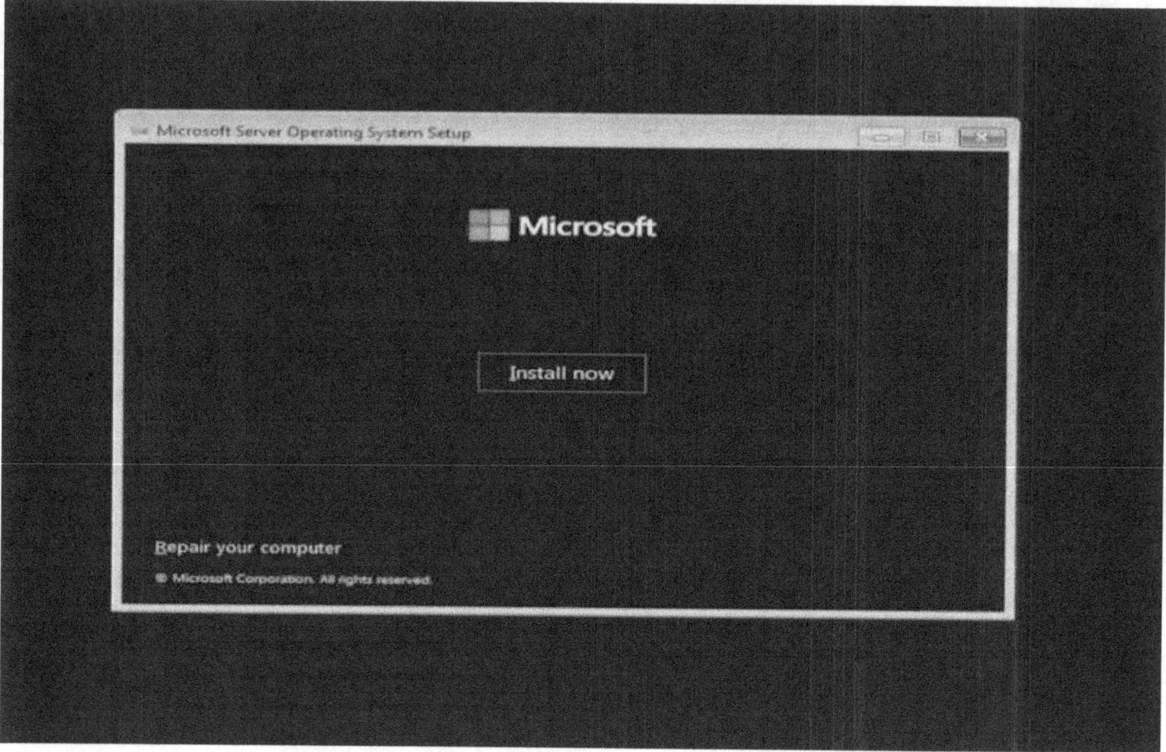

Wait till the setup process is completed.

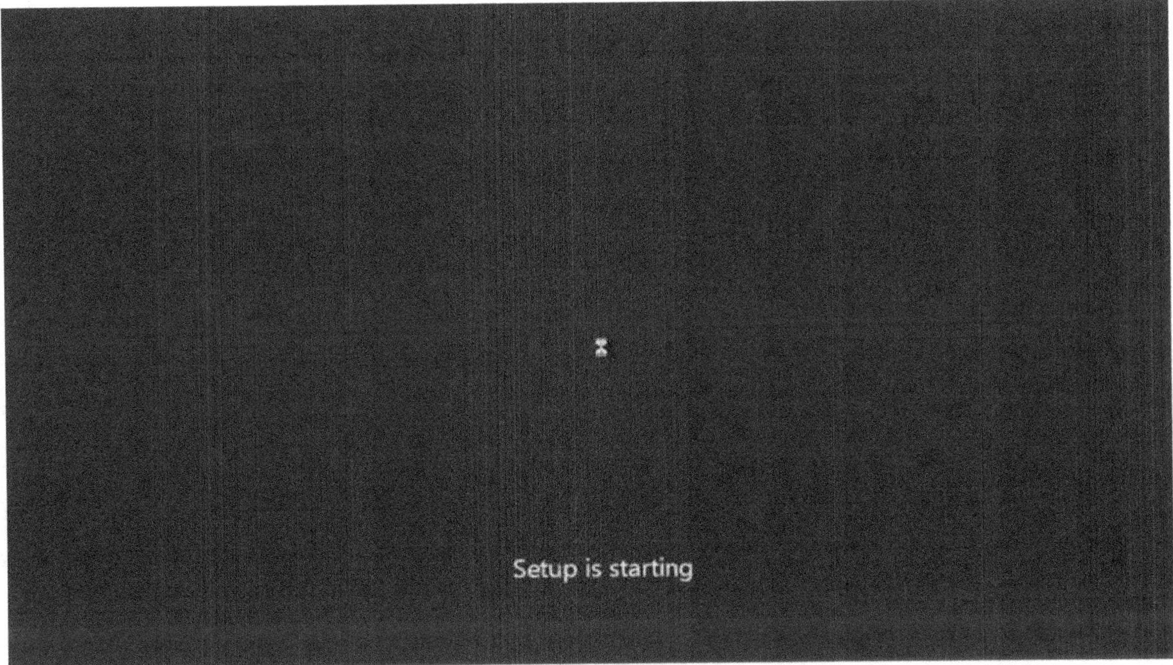

Select the Windows Server 2022 server option with the Server
Core that you want to install in order to get access to and use
some of Microsoft's robust command-line tools. If you prefer to
choose to install Windows Server 2022 using Desktop
Experience, attention to this step carefully till its end.

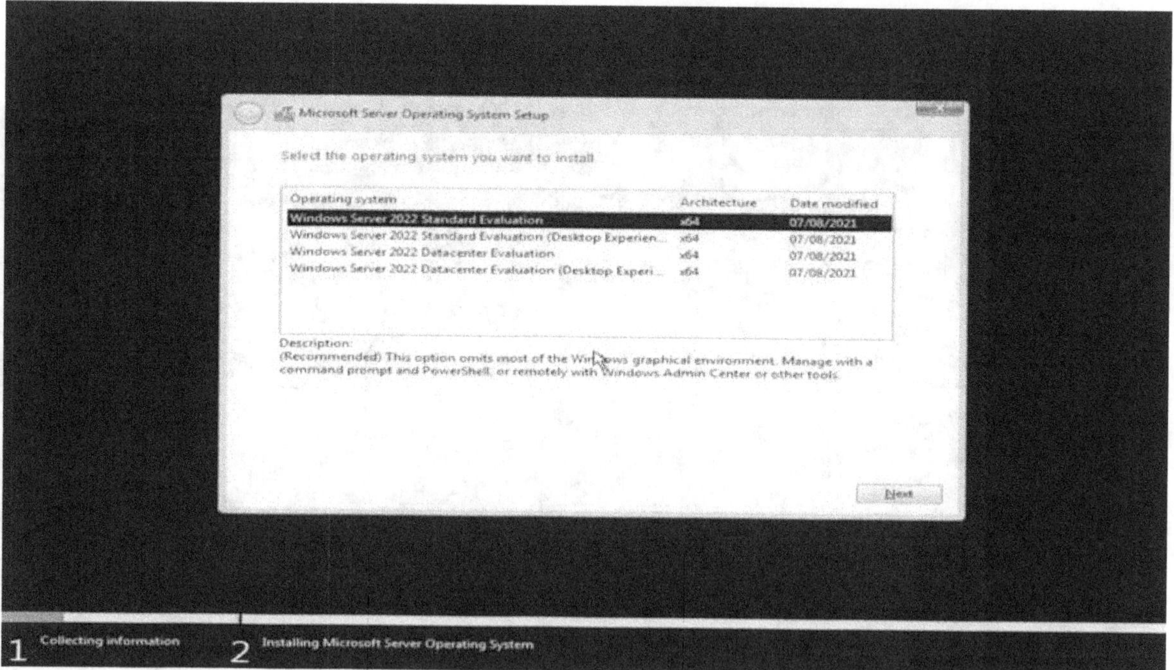

For the installation procedure to proceed, you must read the License terms and tick the "**I accept all license agreements**" box.

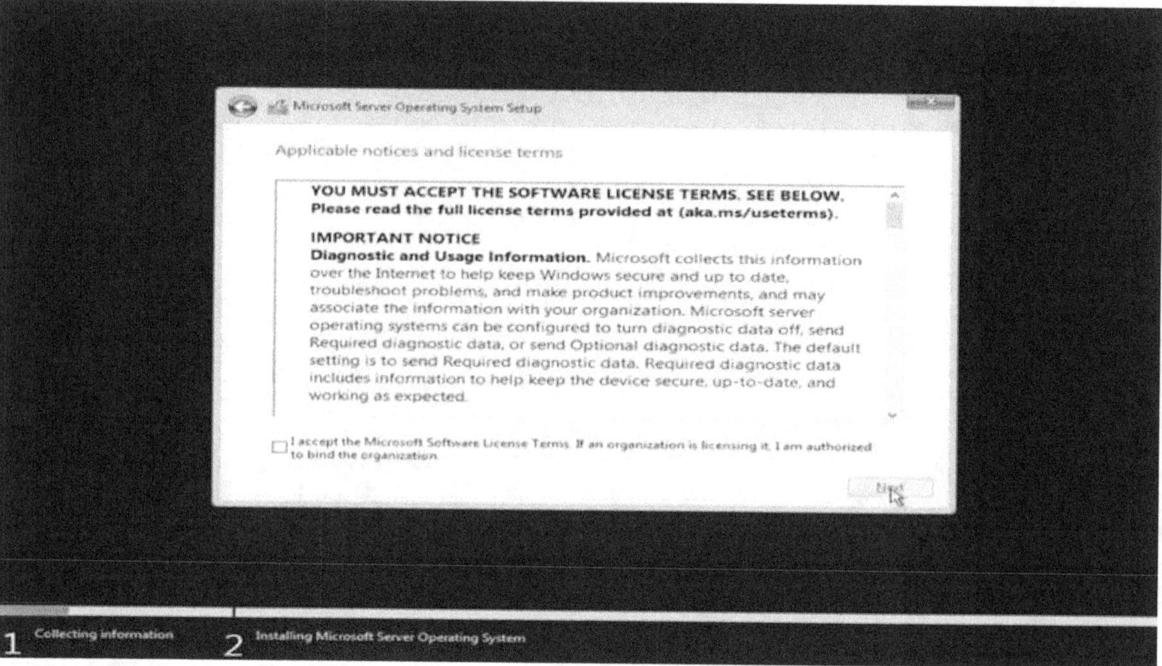

If you're installing the OS on a brand-new server, choose "**Custom: Install Windows Server Operating System only**" while configuring the installation. Otherwise, pick the "**Upgrade: Install Microsoft Server Operating System and keep files, settings, and applications**" option if you're upgrading from a previous version of Windows Server.

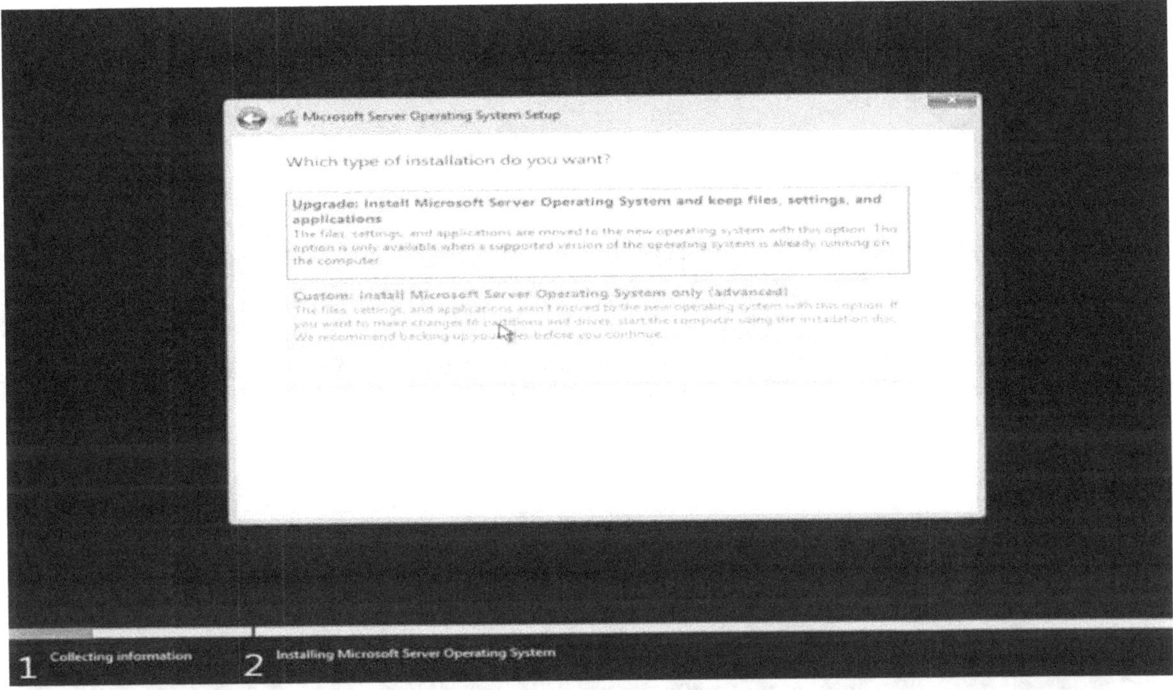

To install Windows Server 2022, choose a partition.

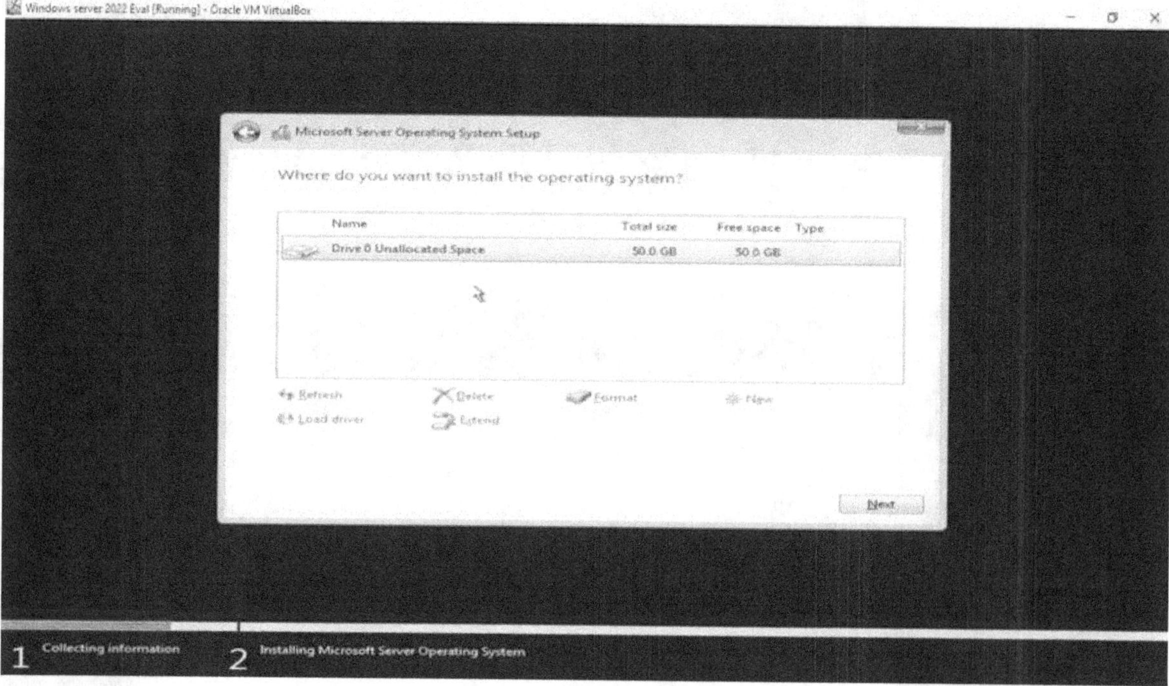

You can decide to use the entire drive size. Otherwise, click on New to make a new considered partition. After making your selection for the OS partition, click "**Next**."

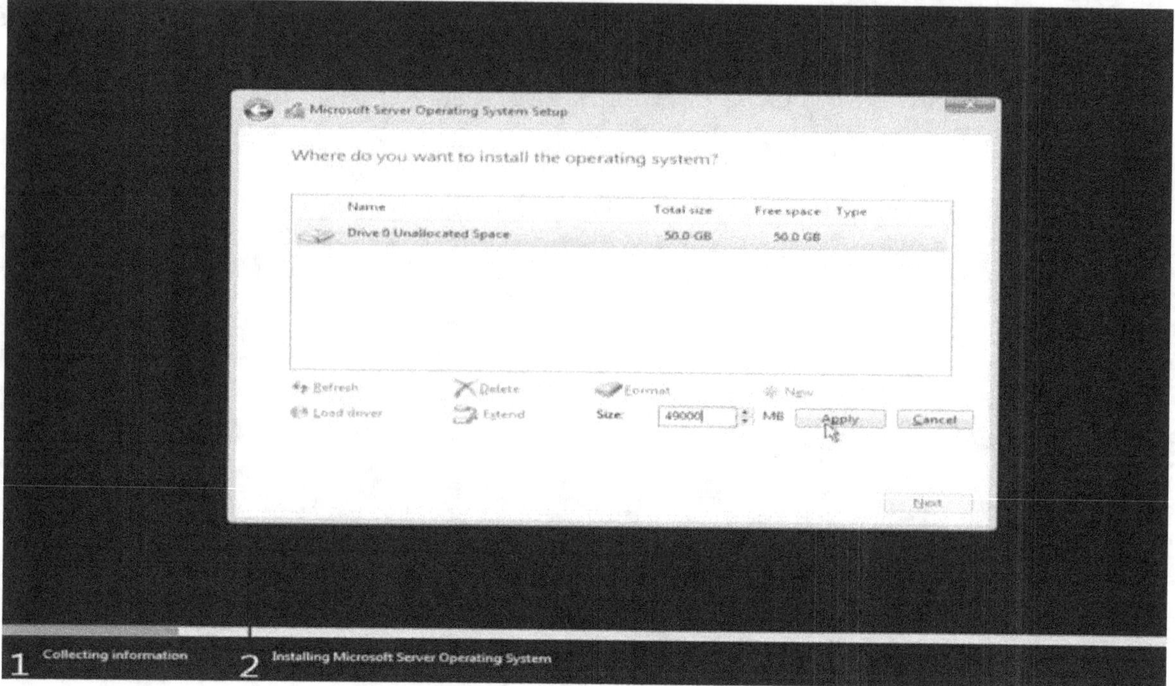

The required system files will start to be installed by the installation. When it is finished, you will see the system reboot on its own.

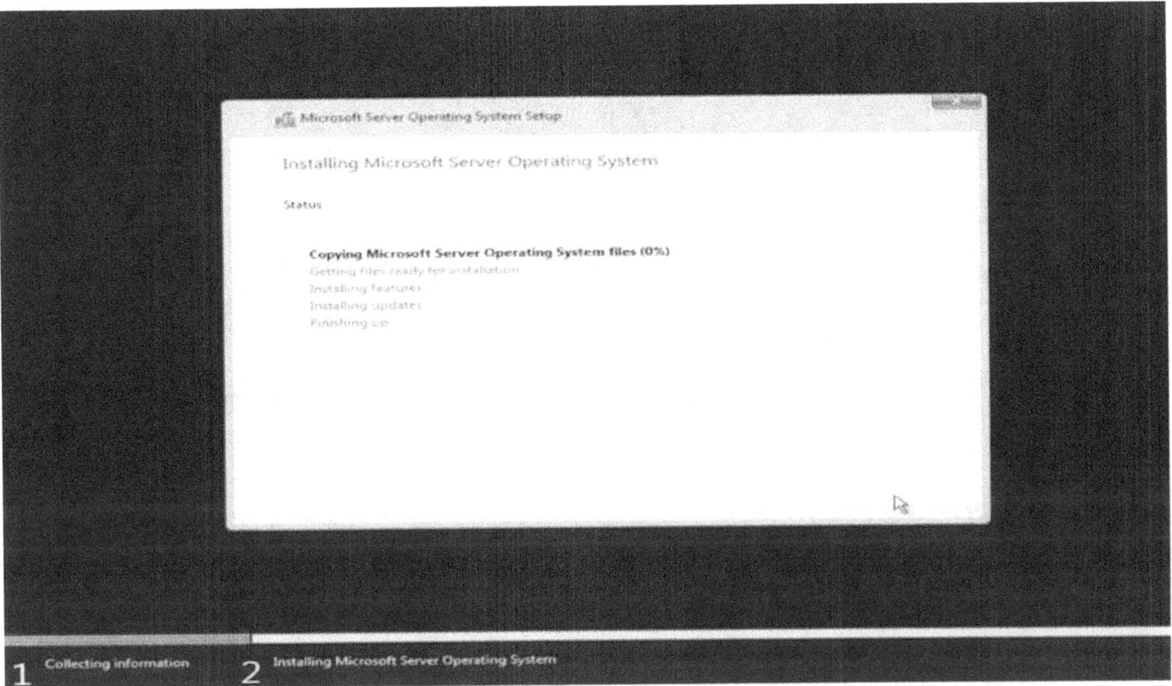

Server management is made simpler by the Desktop Experience installation's specific GUI (Graphical User Interface), which resembles a standard Windows operating system. Once the operating system has been installed and your computer has restarted, continue with the Server Core installation procedures. In addition, be sure to use Windows Server 2022's Desktop Experience option.

Your computer will restart and present you with a graphical user interface. Before continuing, you must first create an administrator password. When finished, click **Finish**.

When you hit **Ctrl + Alt + Del**, the login screen will appear. To access your server again, enter the password that you set up in the previous step.

The Server Manager ought to start up by default.

The Control Panel is available in the same way as it is on conventional Windows operating systems, so you can start customizing your server from here or explore more possibilities there.

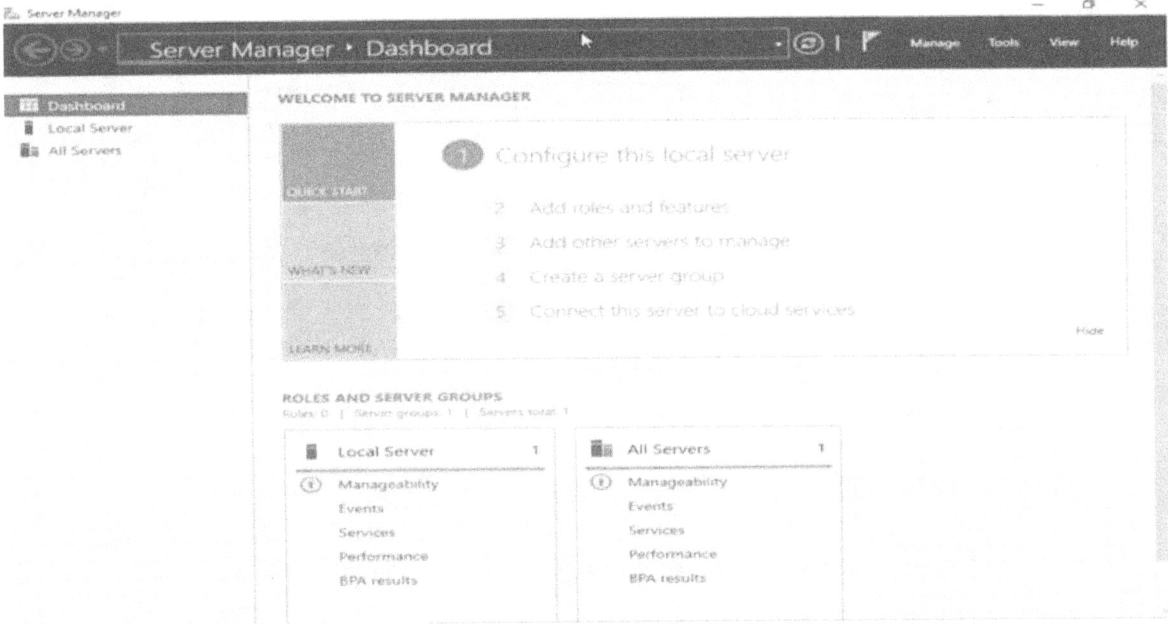

Step 3. Configure Network on Windows Server 2022

So far you reviewed all the required steps to Install Microsoft Windows Server 2022. Let's continue to learn How to Configure your Network on Windows Server 2022. So that system administrators can operate the server remotely and access other areas of their environments, including internet-based services, you must now configure IP addresses and gateway addresses on your network.

1. Windows Server 2022 Server Core

To Configure Network on Windows Server 2022, run the command below in your command prompt area:

SConfig

Once the screen is displayed, choose option 8 for Network Settings to let all the adjustments of wired and wireless networks be configured. Then, just select which IP (or IPs) you need to configure. If your server has more than one network, you must see multiple options. You can start adjusting your settings after choosing your IP for configuration. The network settings on the machine will be changed automatically. It should just take five minutes to complete the process.

2. Windows Server 2022 Desktop Experience

If you have chosen to install Windows Server 2022 with a desktop experience, follow the below instructions to do Network configuration on it.

1. By clicking the magnifying glass icon in your taskbar, you may access the **Search** interface. Additionally, you can access it by pressing **Windows + S** on your keyboard.

2. Enter "**Control Panel**" into the search box, then select the first result that matches. Go to **Network and Internet** > **Network Connections** when it opens.

3. Select with a **right-click** the network you wish to customize. In our case, we just have one network connection to the server computer, but there may be more alternatives available to you. Choose **Properties** from the context menu after selecting the item you want to configure.

The GUI, which mimics Windows 10's, can be used to start configuring the network connection.

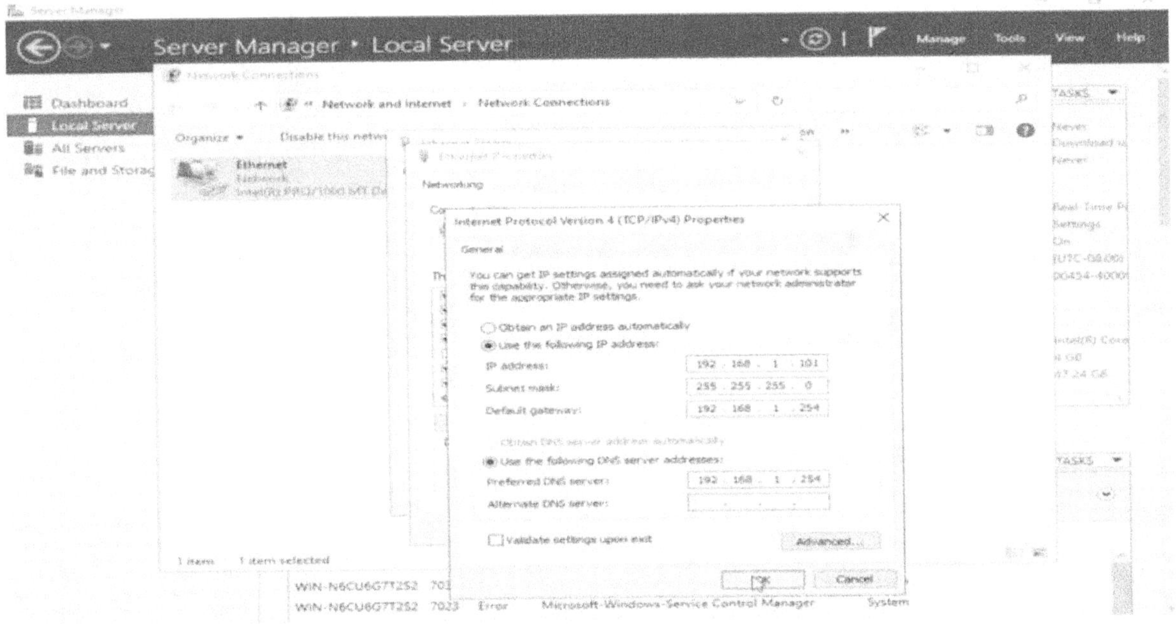

How to Install Windows Server 2022 Without Error?

As you know, a Dedicated server is a requirement for installing Windows Server. Since the support team of your provider does not install Windows Server 2022, you need to use virtual machines such as esxi or kvm.

Installing Windows Server on a PC also requires a virtual machine which seems difficult for many users. So, what is the OperaVPS team's suggestion? You can easily buy Windows VPS with a pre-installed Windows Server 2022 to not have to do all the required steps of installation and manage the long process of installation.

CHAPTER 3: Install Active Directory Domain Services in Windows Server 2022

One of the most illustrious product that makes Windows server to shine in the Enterprise sphere is Active Directory. This single Sign-on product seems to seamlessly and easily integrate with most of Microsoft and non-Microsoft products making user management among other tasks quite easy and fun. This guide is about how to install Active Directory Domain Services on a newly installed Windows server 2022. In case you would like to install it in Windows Server 2019, check out Install Active Directory Domain Services in Windows Server 2019. Let us follow the following steps to get AD installed.

Step 1: Open Server Manager

Hit "*Windows*" key on your keyboard and type "*Server Manager*" to search for the application. Once it is open as illustrated by the figure below, let us now proceed to the next step of installing *Active Directory Domain Services*.

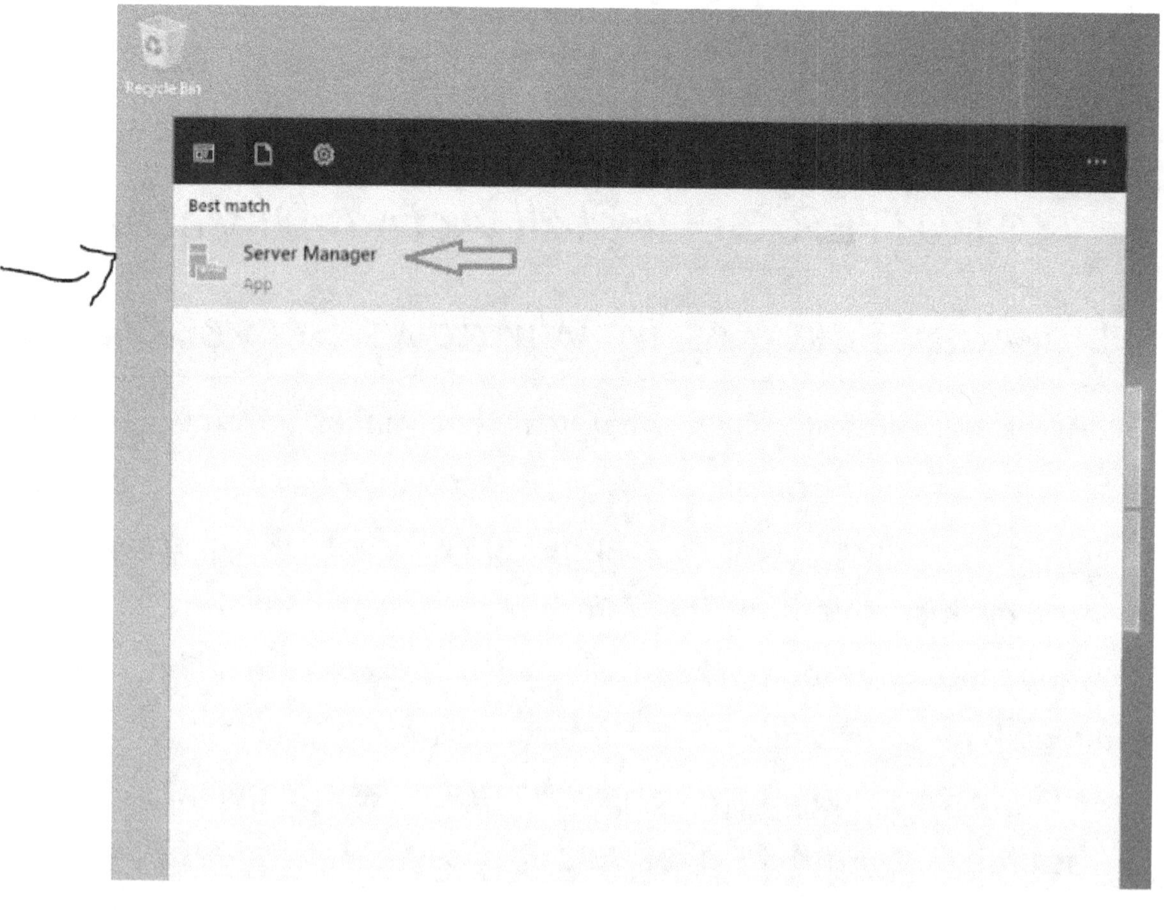

Step 2: Add Roles and Features

Right-click on "**Manage**" on the "**Server Manager**" window and choose "**Add Roles and Features**".

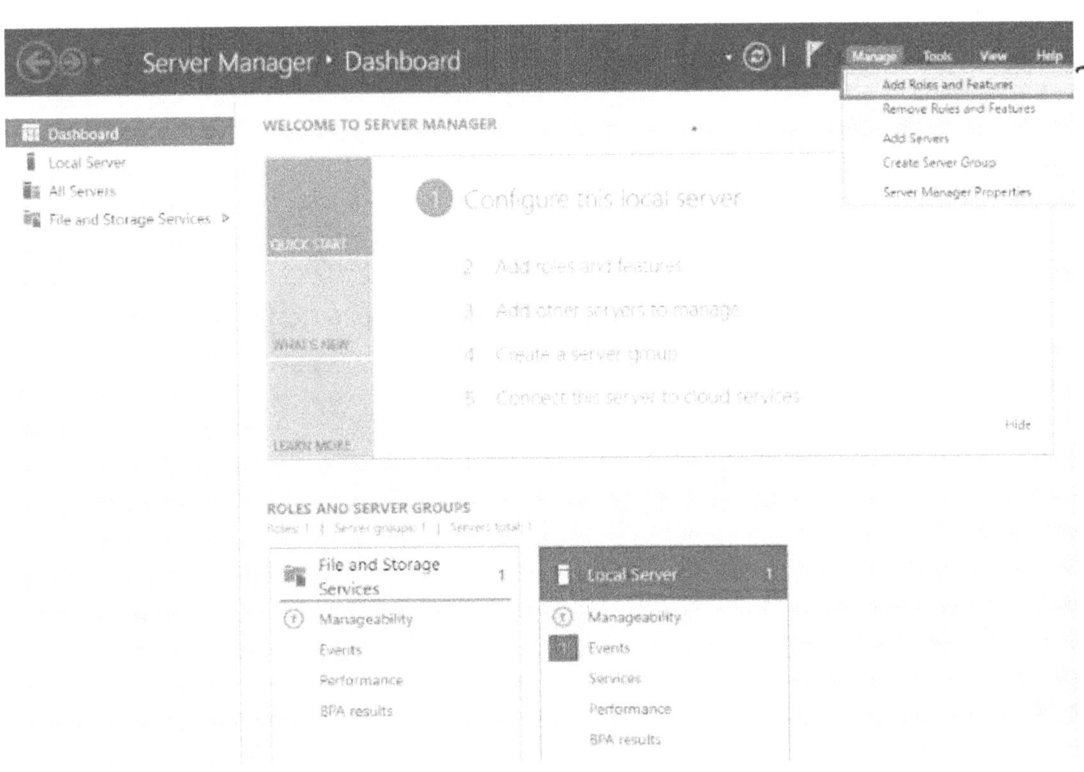

This will open the "***Add Roles and Features Wizard***" which ushers us to the part where we install Active Directory Domain Services. Click on **next**.

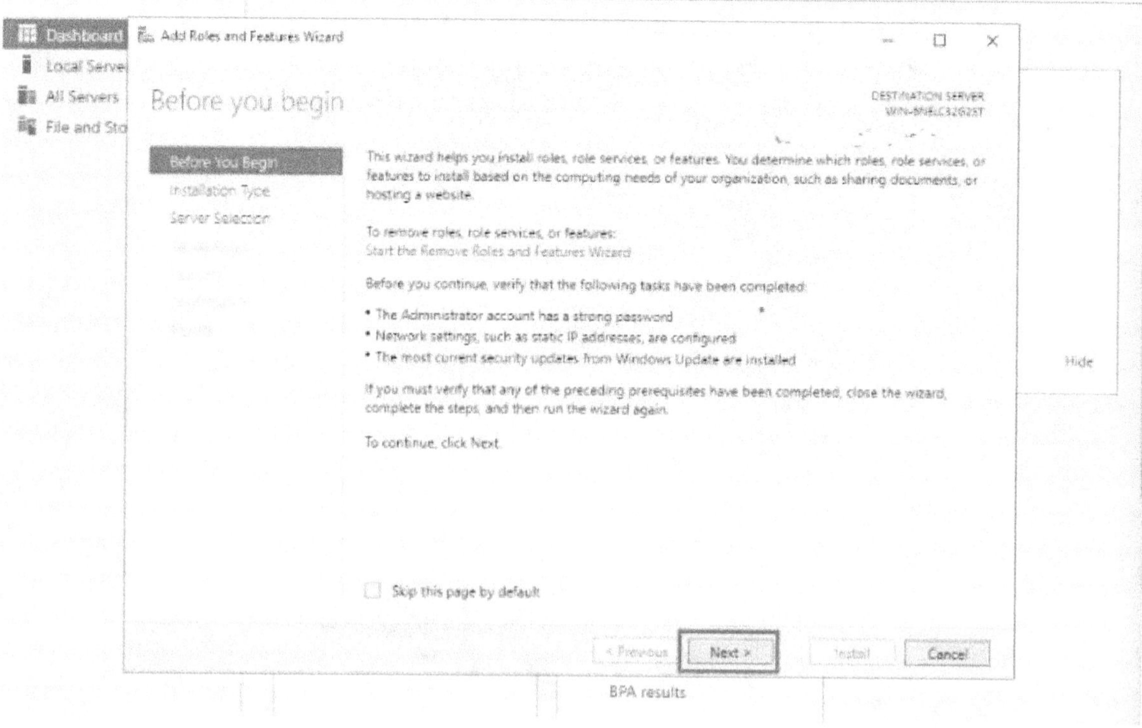

Step 3: Installation Type

On the "*Installation Type*", leave "*Role-based or feature-based installation*" radio button selected and click on next.

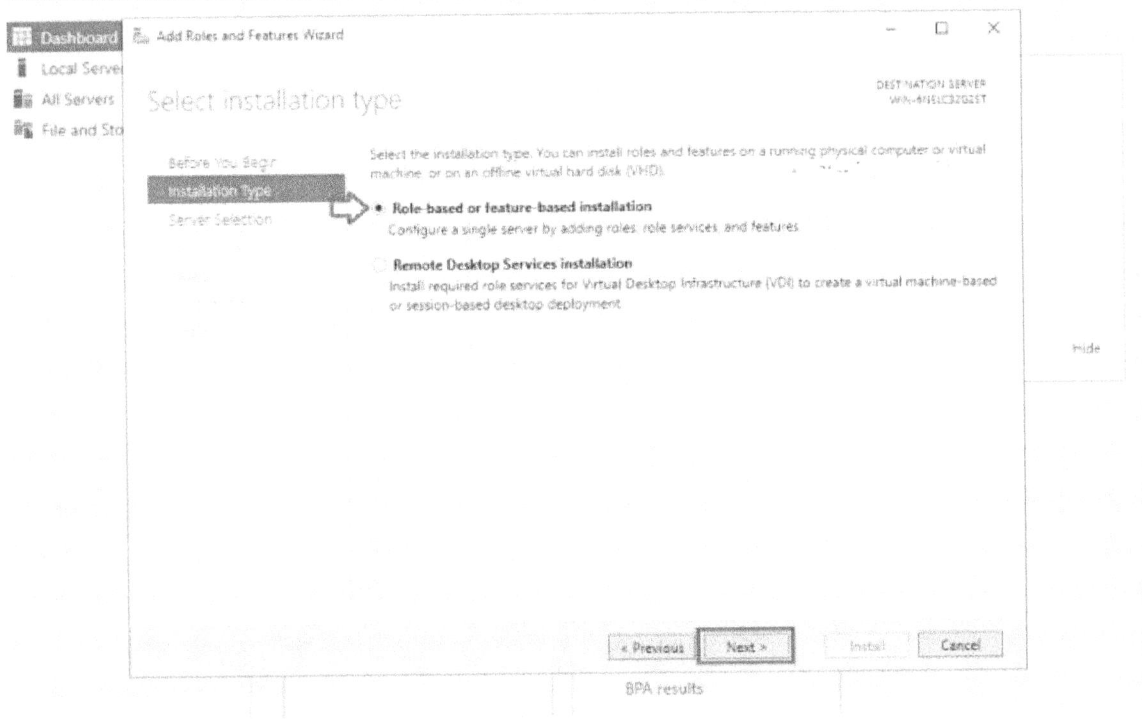

Step 4: Server Selection

On this stage titled "*Select destination server*", select the server you are to install AD DS and click next. I am going to choose my local server which is Windows Server 2022 evaluation as you can observe below.

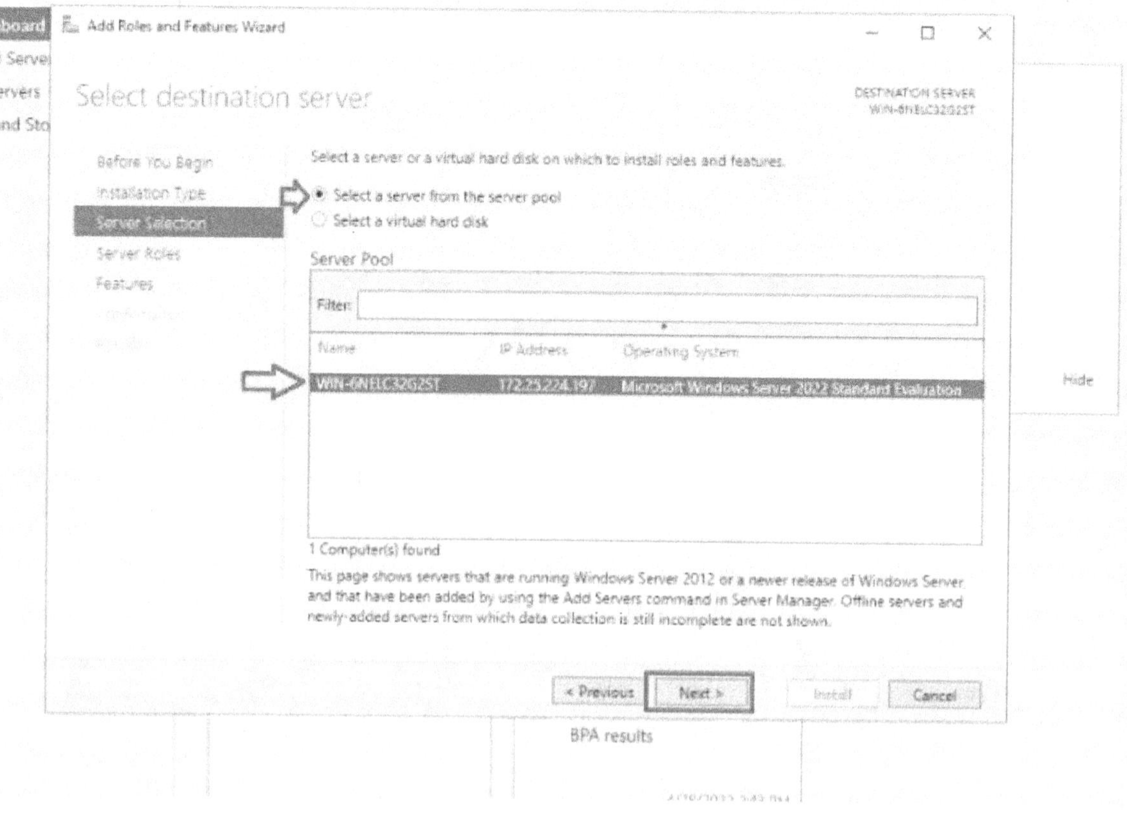

Step 5: Server Roles

The previous step will lead you to the next page as shown below.
Here, you will see many options with square checklist box against
them. As you can guess, we are going to choose "***Active
Directory Domain Services***".

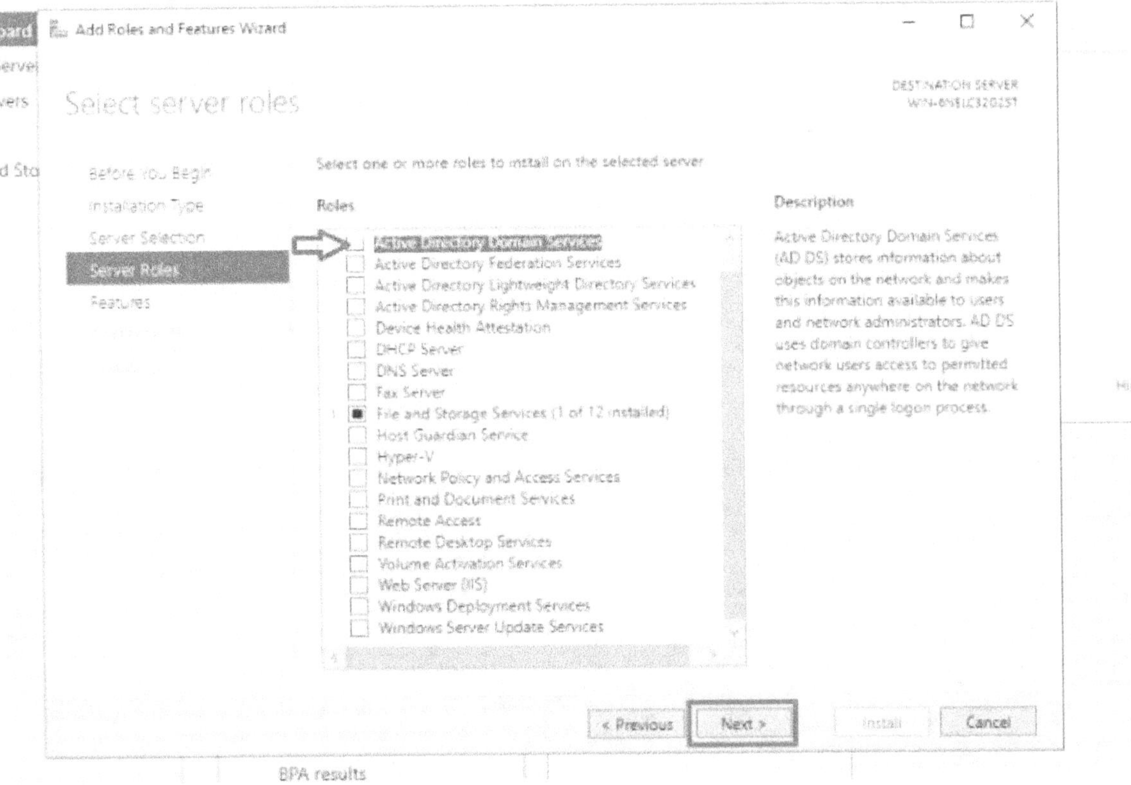

Step 6: Add Features

Immediately you choose that option, a new part comes up. On the page, just click on "**Add Features**" tab and hit "**Next**".

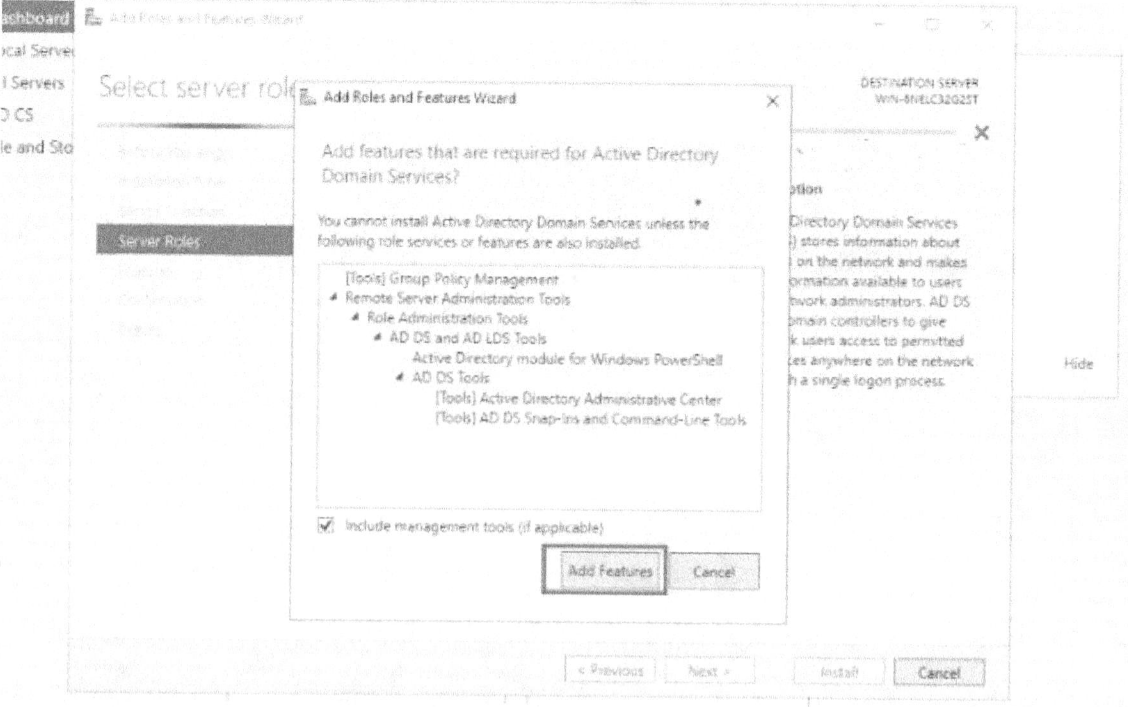

Step 7: Select Features

On the next page after Step 6 titled "**Select features**", just hit "**Next**" to lead you to "Active Directory Domain Services" page.

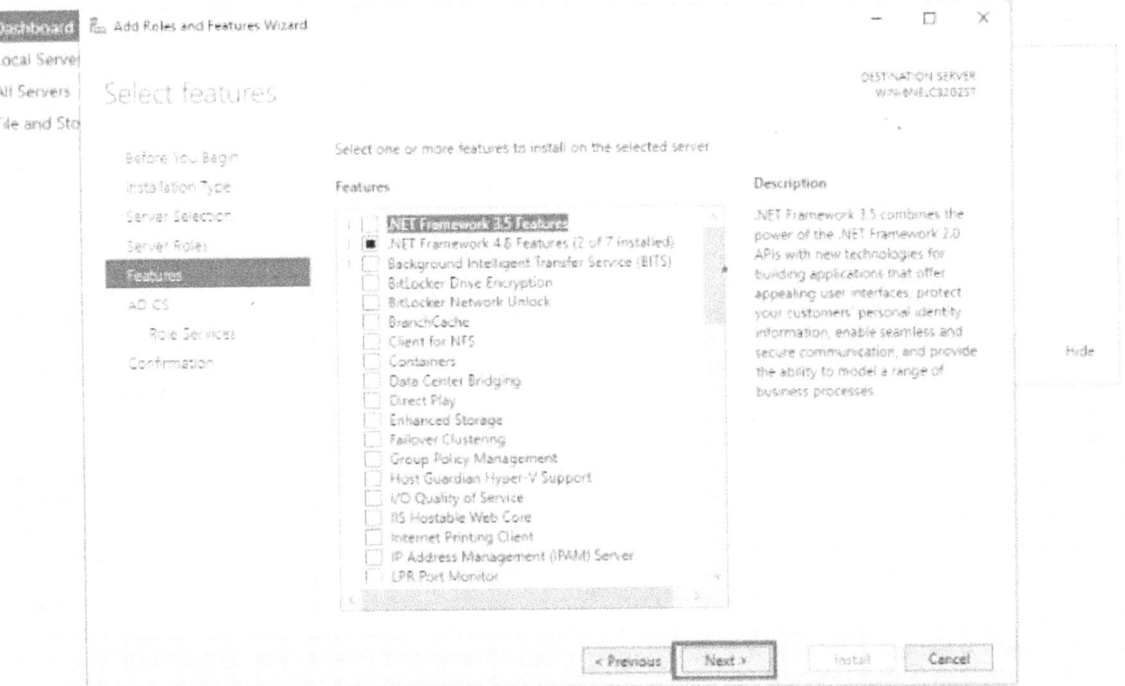

Step 8: AD DS

As shown below, you will be presented with the next page titled "*Active Directory Domain Services*". Here, click on "*Next*"

Step 9: Confirm your selections

The next page is about Confirming what you need to install before actually installing them. If you are sure about what you have chosen, click on install. You can optionally choose the option that restarts the server whenever required.

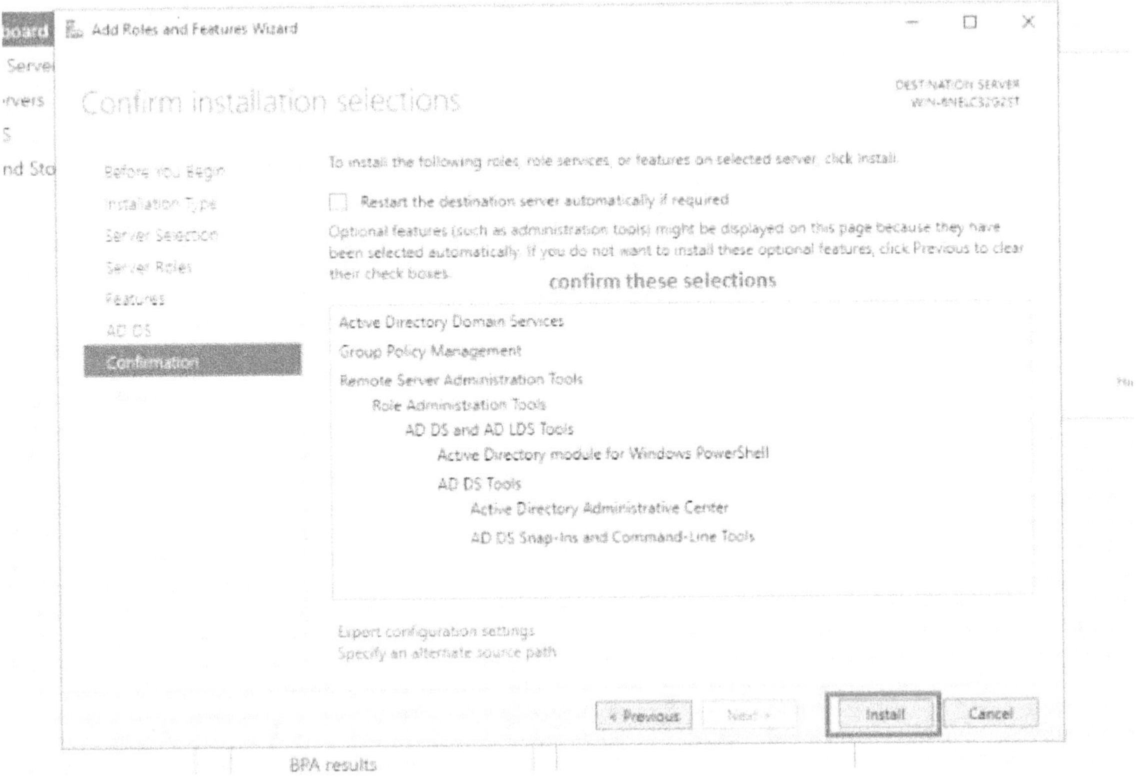

Installation Progress

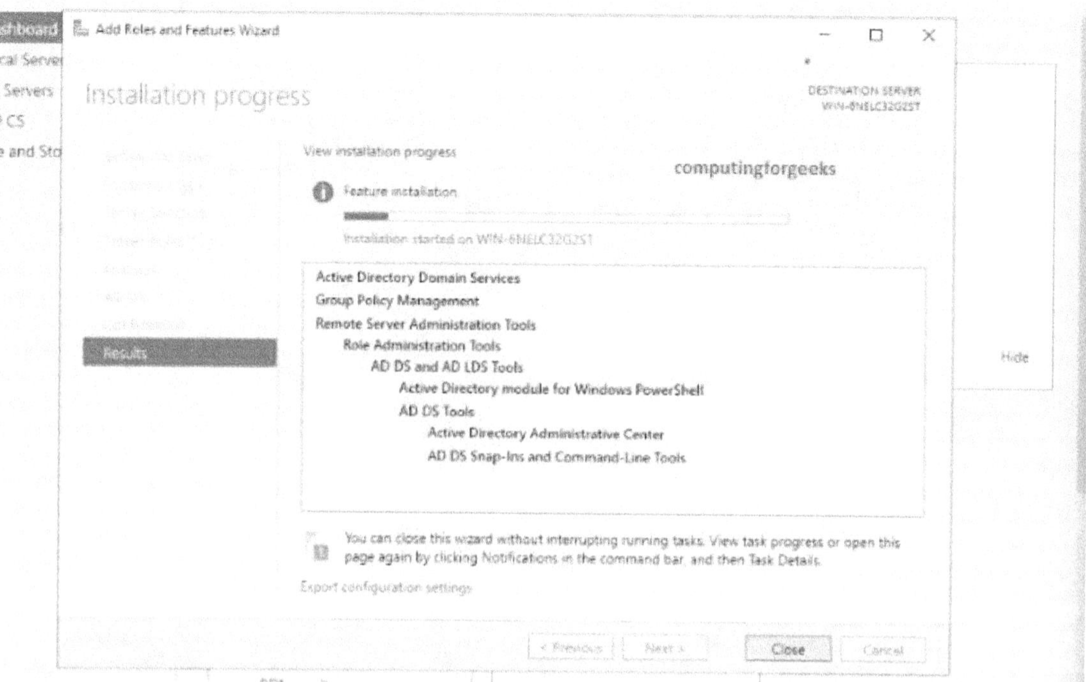

Click on "***Close***" once it is done.

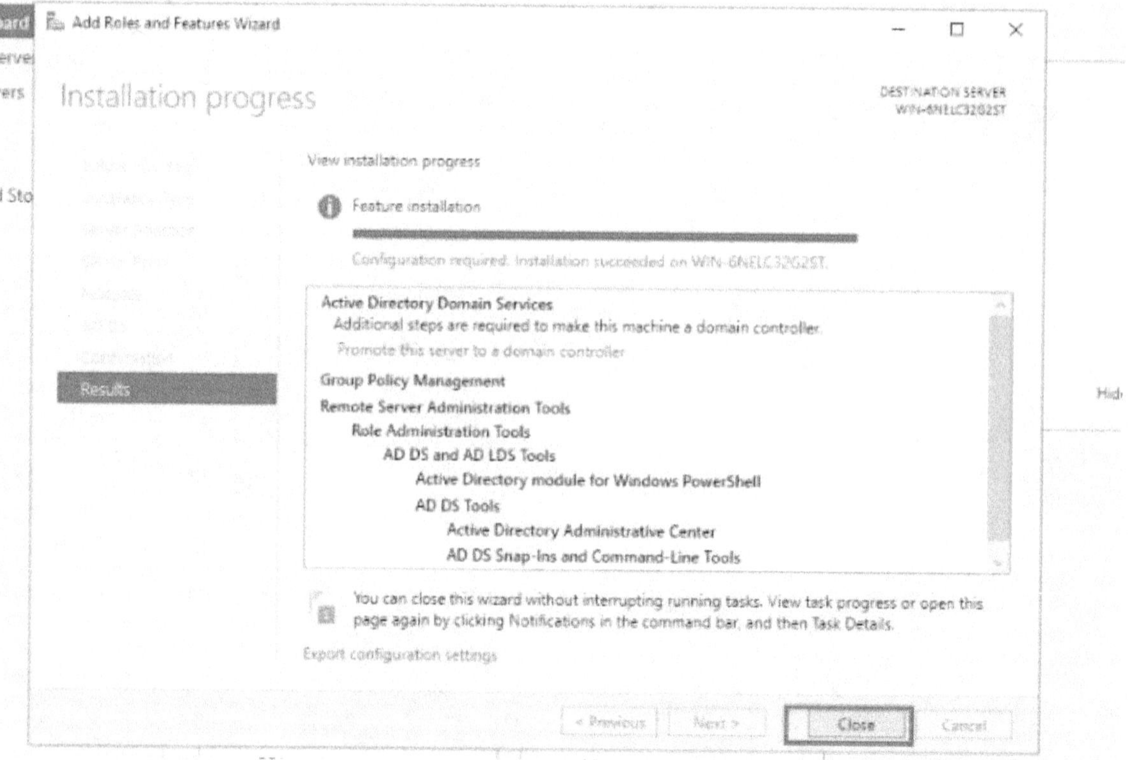

Step 10: Promote to Domain Controller Post Installation Configuration

After you have finished installing Active Directory Domain Services, the last step is to promote it to a Domain Controller. Go over to Server Manager where you will notice a yellow exclamation notification beside the "**Manage**" tab as shown below. Click on it and choose "**Promote this server to a domain controller**"

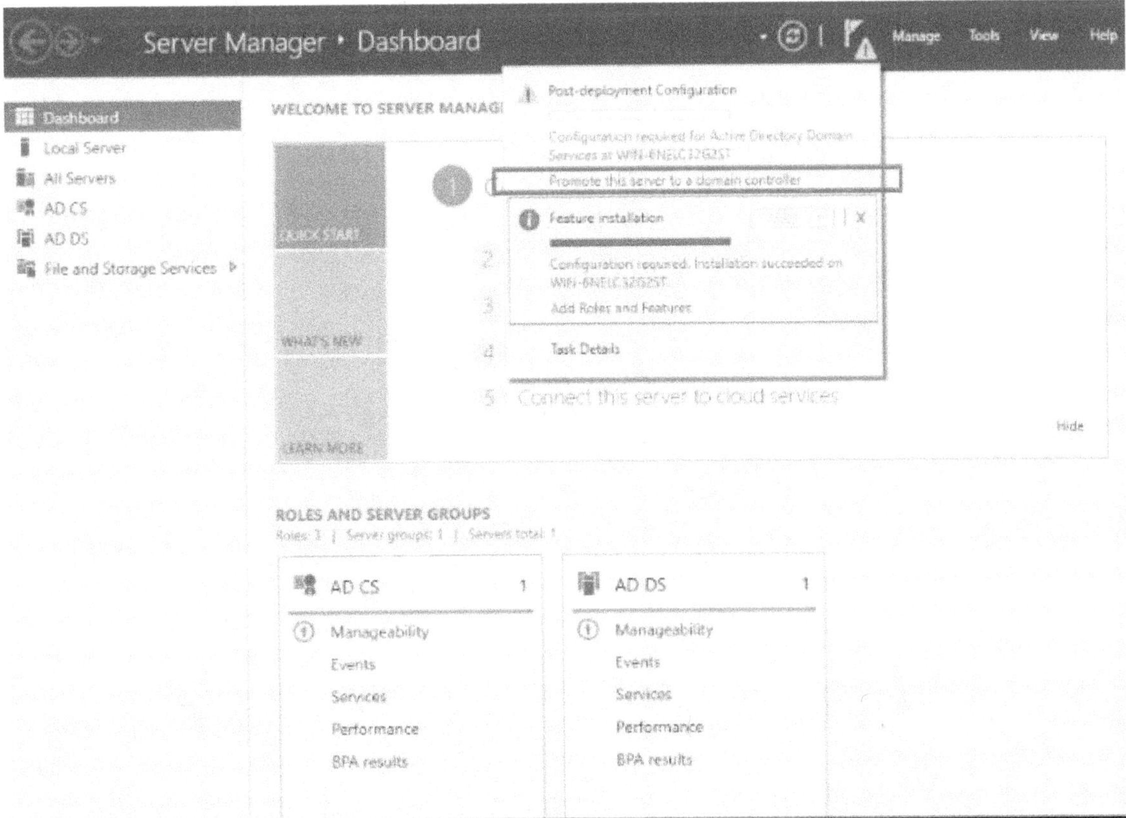

Step 11: Add a new Forest

A new window titled "***Active Directory Domain Services Configuration Wizard***" as shown below will pop up. We are going to **Add a new Forest** but in case you would wish to do something different in this Step, you are free to choose the other options. Add your organization's root domain name. Click on "***Next***" after you pick your choice.

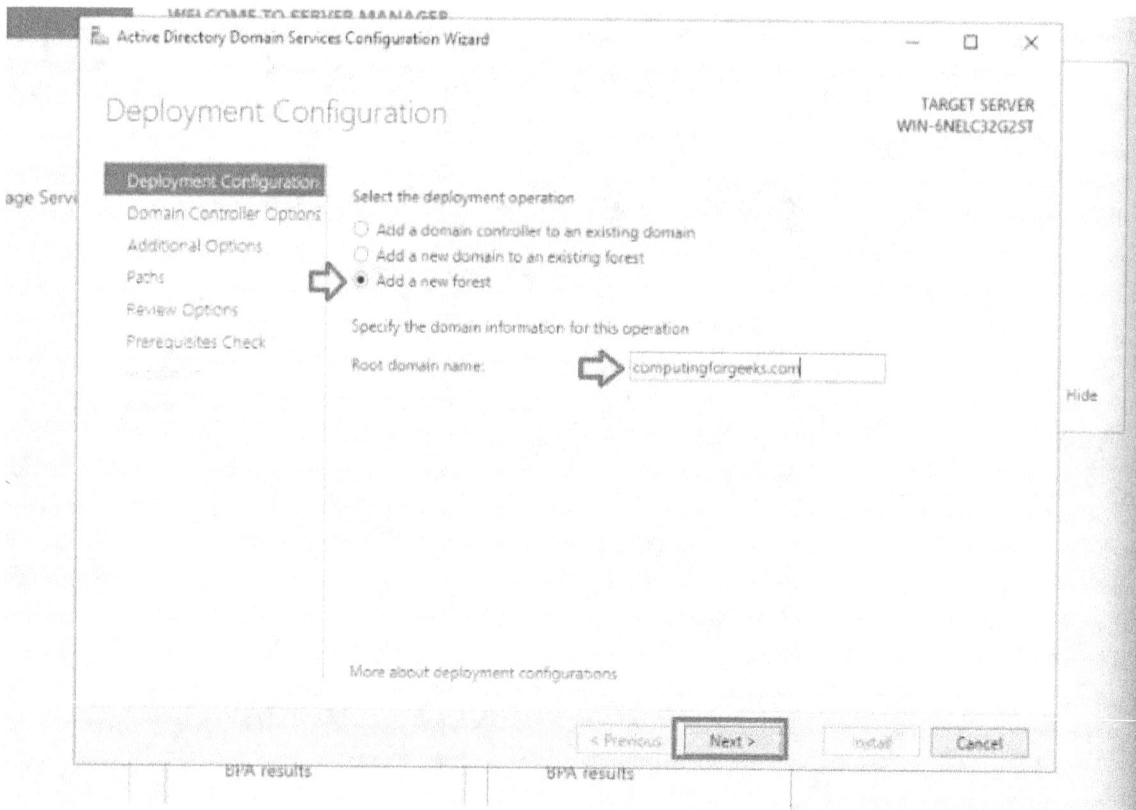

Step 12: Domain Controller Options

On the Domain Controller options, leave the defaults checked
and input your password. Once done, click "*Next*".

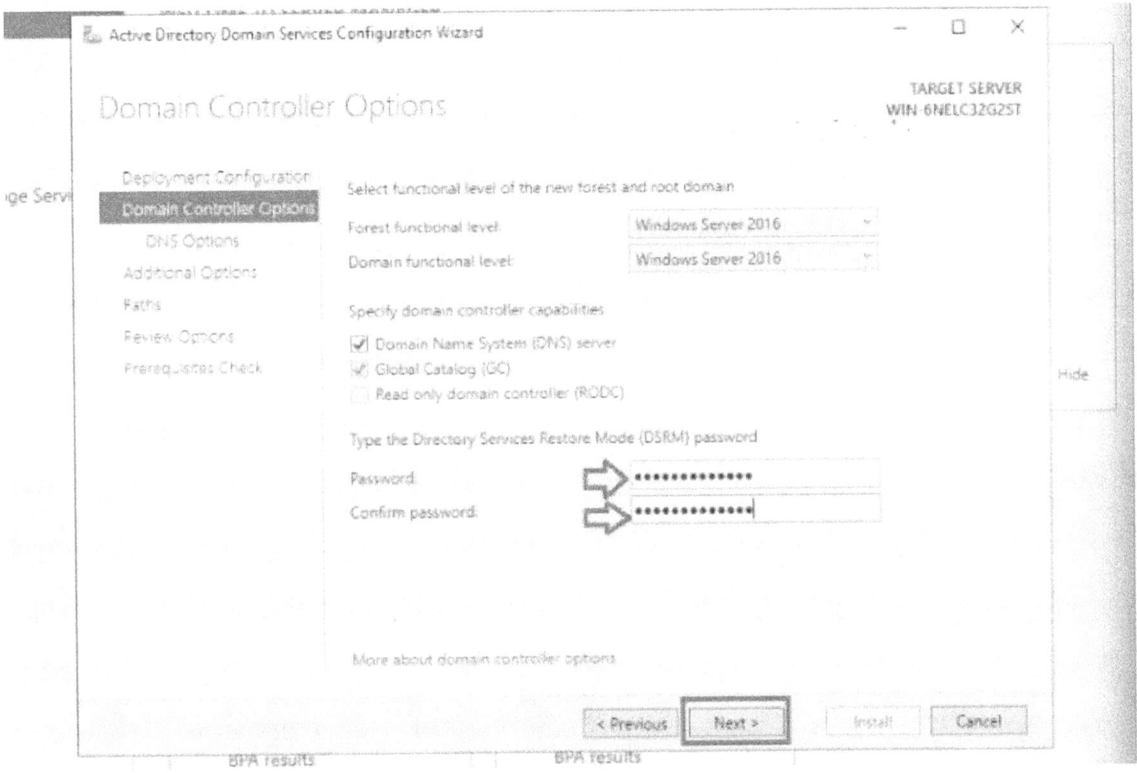

Step 13: DNS Options

On the next page (DNS Options), you will probably see an error
on top with the words "*A delegation for this DNS server cannot
be created because the authoritative parent zone nameserver
cannot be found*". Ignore it and click "*Next*".

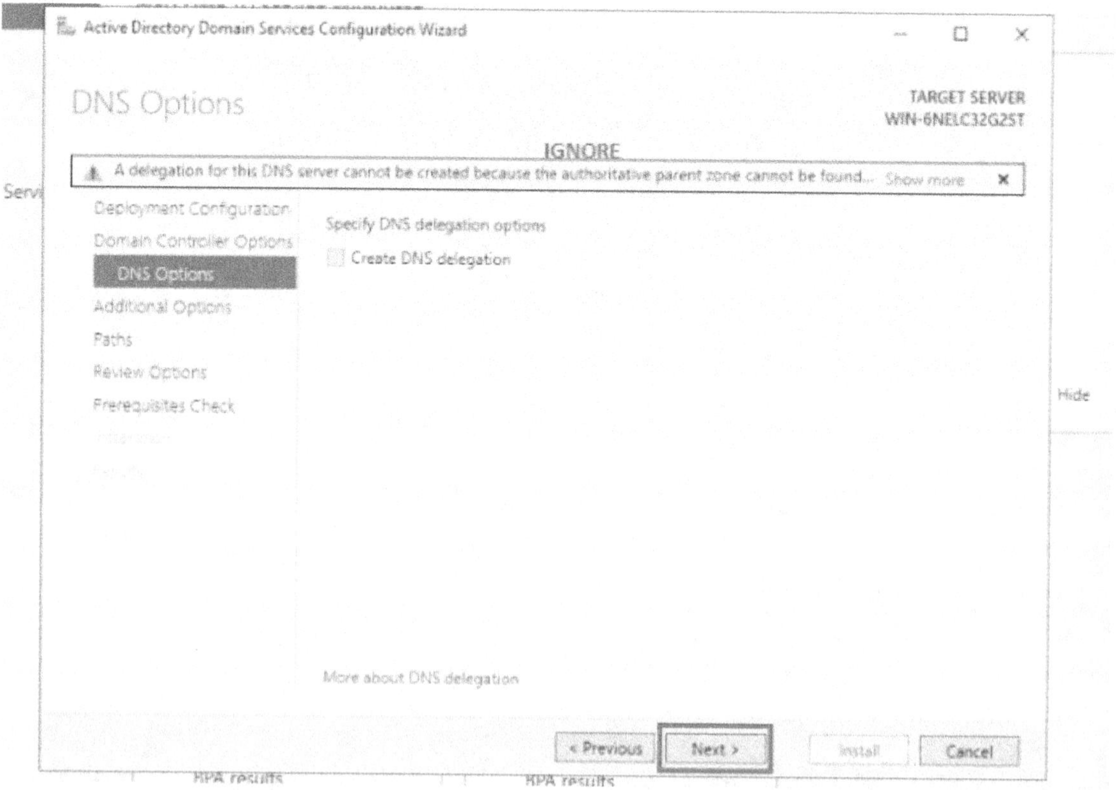

Step 14: NetBIOS domain name

On the next page, leave the NetBIOS domain name as default or you can change it as long as it is not longer than 15 characters. Click "*Next*" after that.

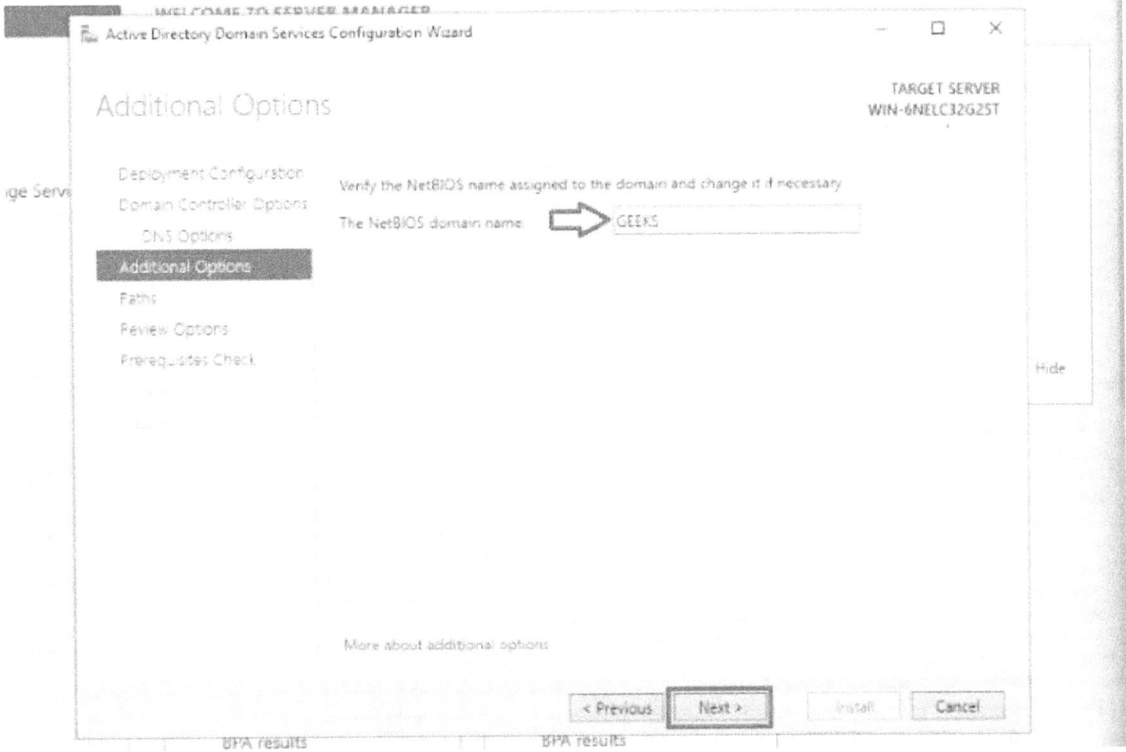

Step 15: Paths

Leave paths as default and click "*Next*" as shown below.

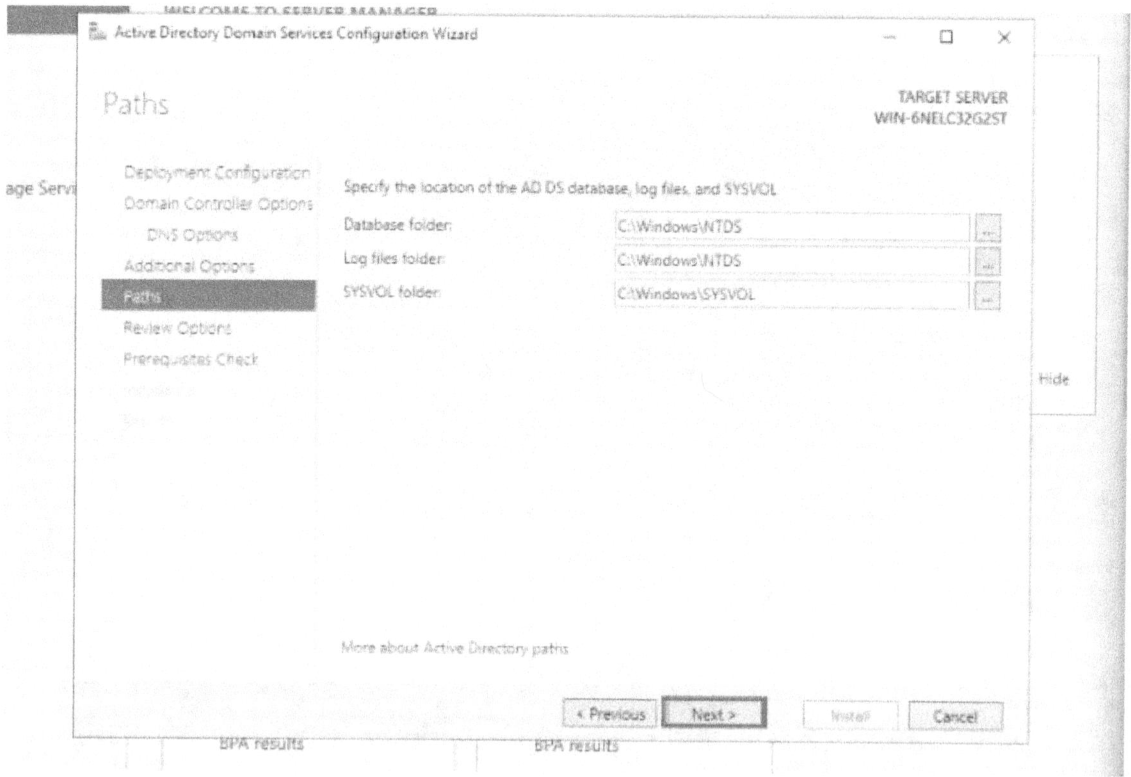

Step 16: Review Selections

In this step, the server allows you to review what you have done so far. If you are good with the selections you have done. Hit "*Next*".

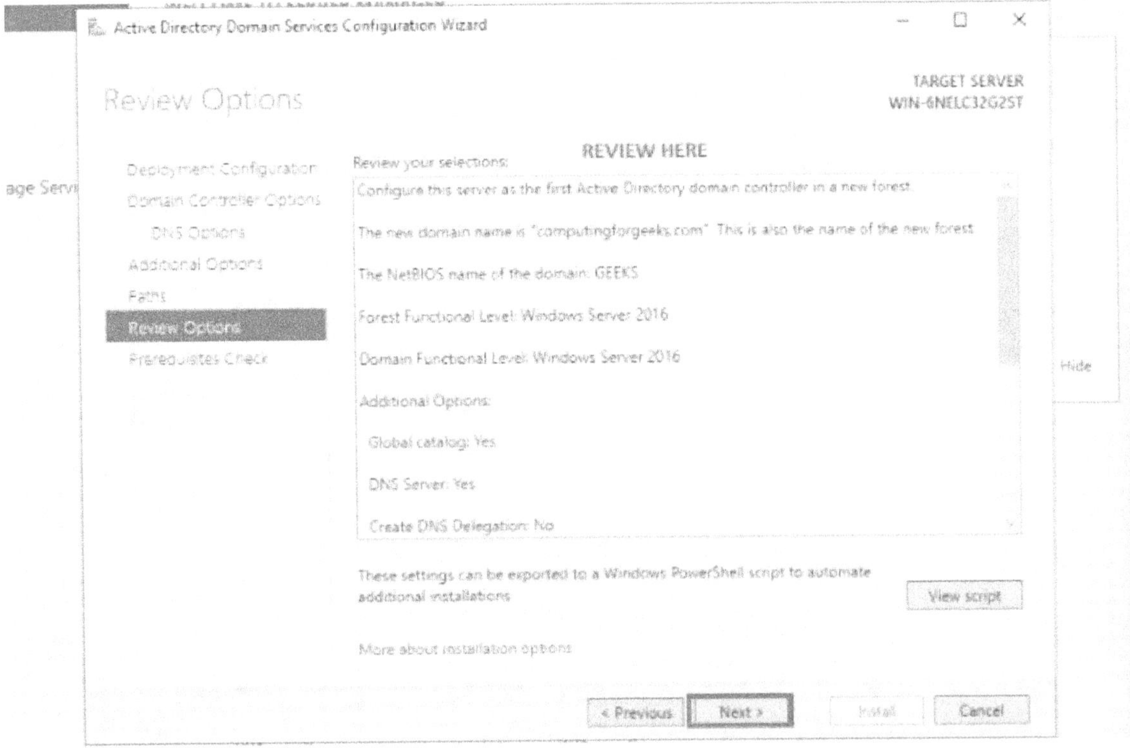

Step 17: Pre-requisites Check

In this step prerequisites will be validated before Active Directory
Domain Services is installed. If you get any errors here, please
look at it and fix anything in the previous steps. If all is okay,
click "*Install*".

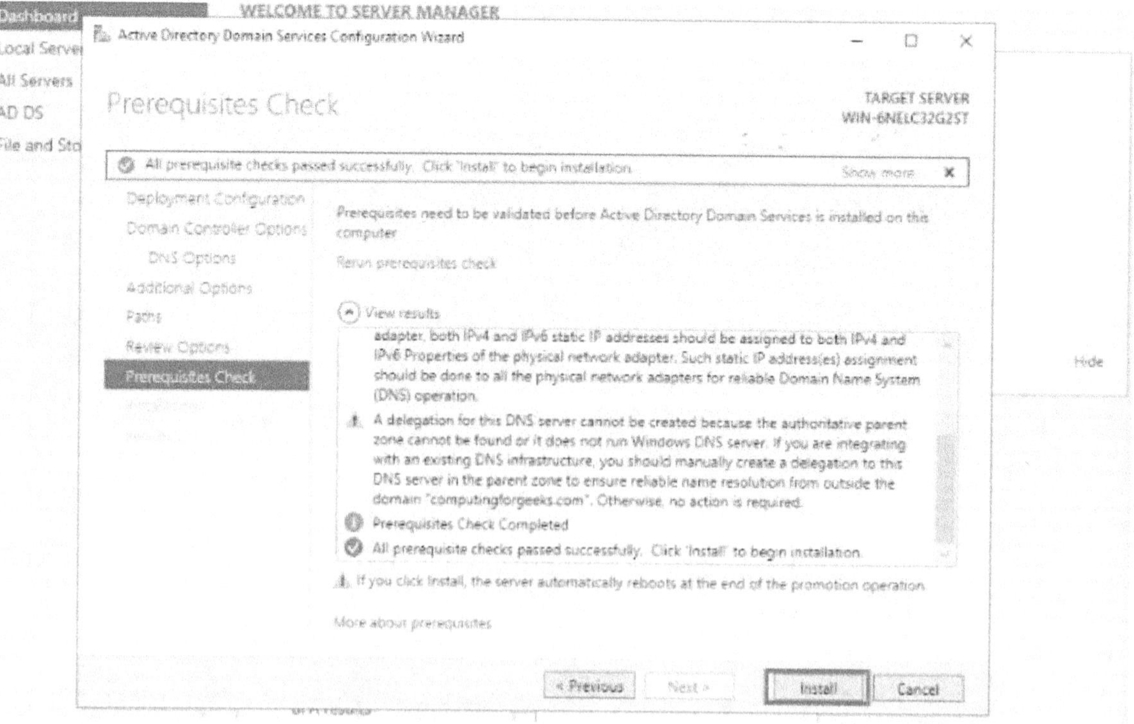

After that, the Server will reboot and you can then log into the Domain with the credentials you set in "*Step 12*" as shown below:

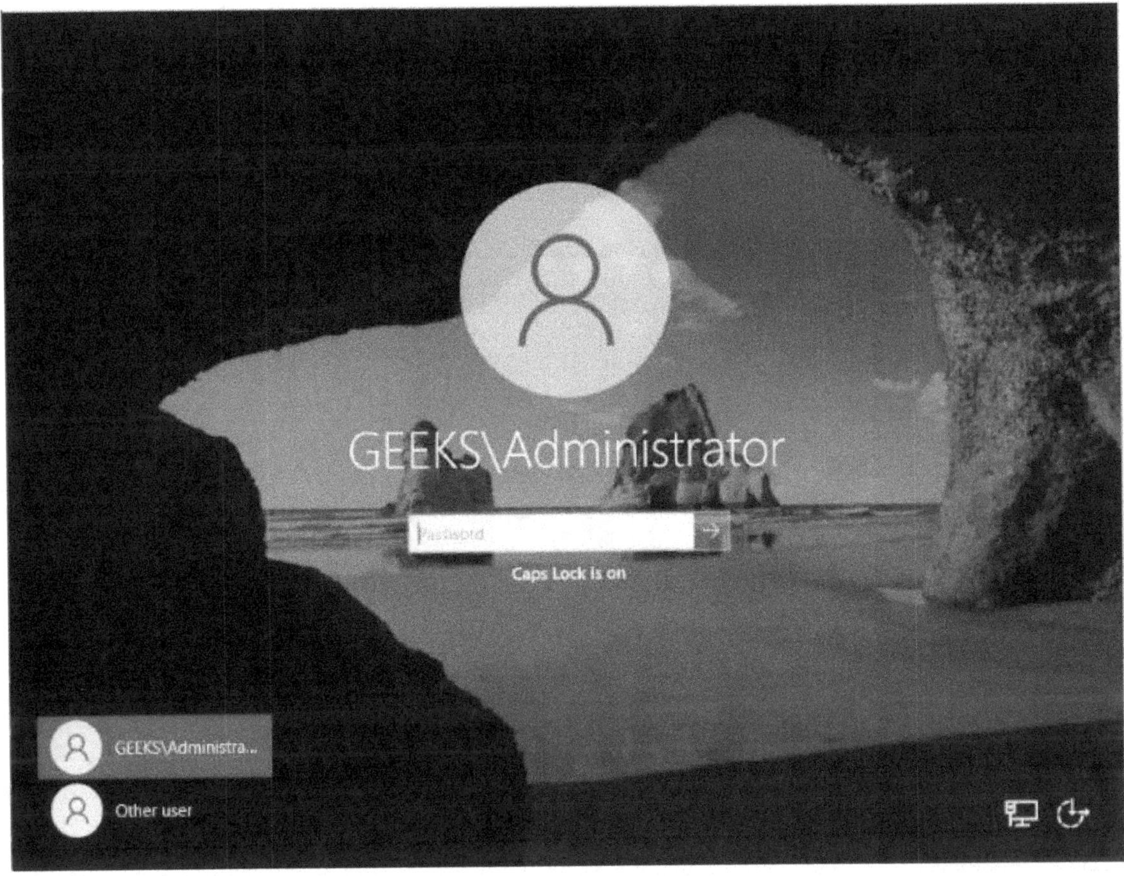

Concluding Remarks

With the new Windows server 2022, you now have Active Directory Domain Services Installed and can be managed by Active Directory Administrative Center. Many tools you have in your organization can be integrated with it so that you have an easy time managing users in all of them. We hope the guide was as clear and informative as we wished. All in all, we truly hope and you enjoyed.

CHAPTER 4 : Create Users and Groups on Active Directory – Windows Server 2022

The user represents a real user who is part of an organization's AD network. Group is an object that can contain other AD objects such as other groups, users, and computers, Hence, a group object is a container object. This step-by-step tutorial covers how to Create Users and Groups on Active Directory.

Table of Contents

- Create User on Active Directory – Windows Server 2022
- Create Group on Active Directory – Windows Server 2022

Prerequisite Required

- Install and configure Active Directory Domain Services

Demo environment

- Computer Name: server1.test.com
- Operating System: Windows Server 2022 Datacenter
- IP Address: 192.168.0.3

Create User on Active Directory – Windows Server 2022

In this step, we are going to create a user (user1@test.com)

1. Open Server Manager, click Tools and select Active Directory Users and Computer.

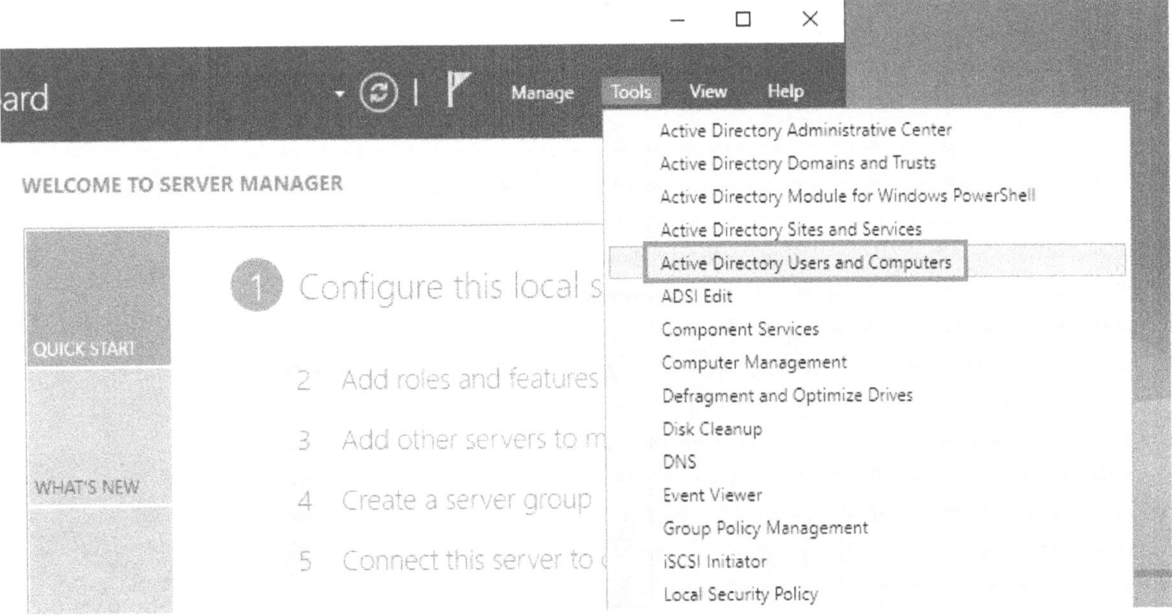

2. Right-click on Users, click New and select User.

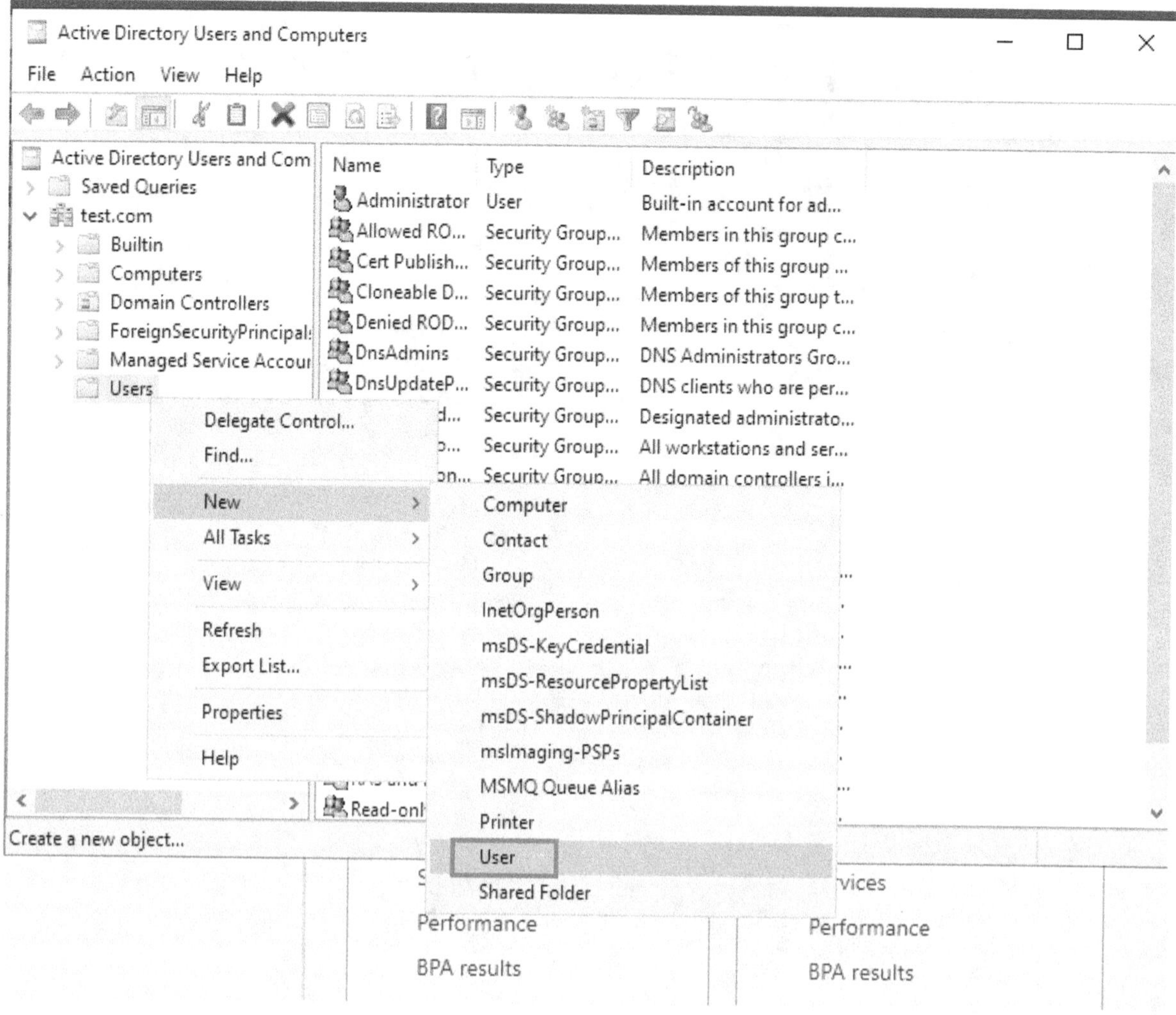

3. Enter the Name and User login name for a new user and click Next.

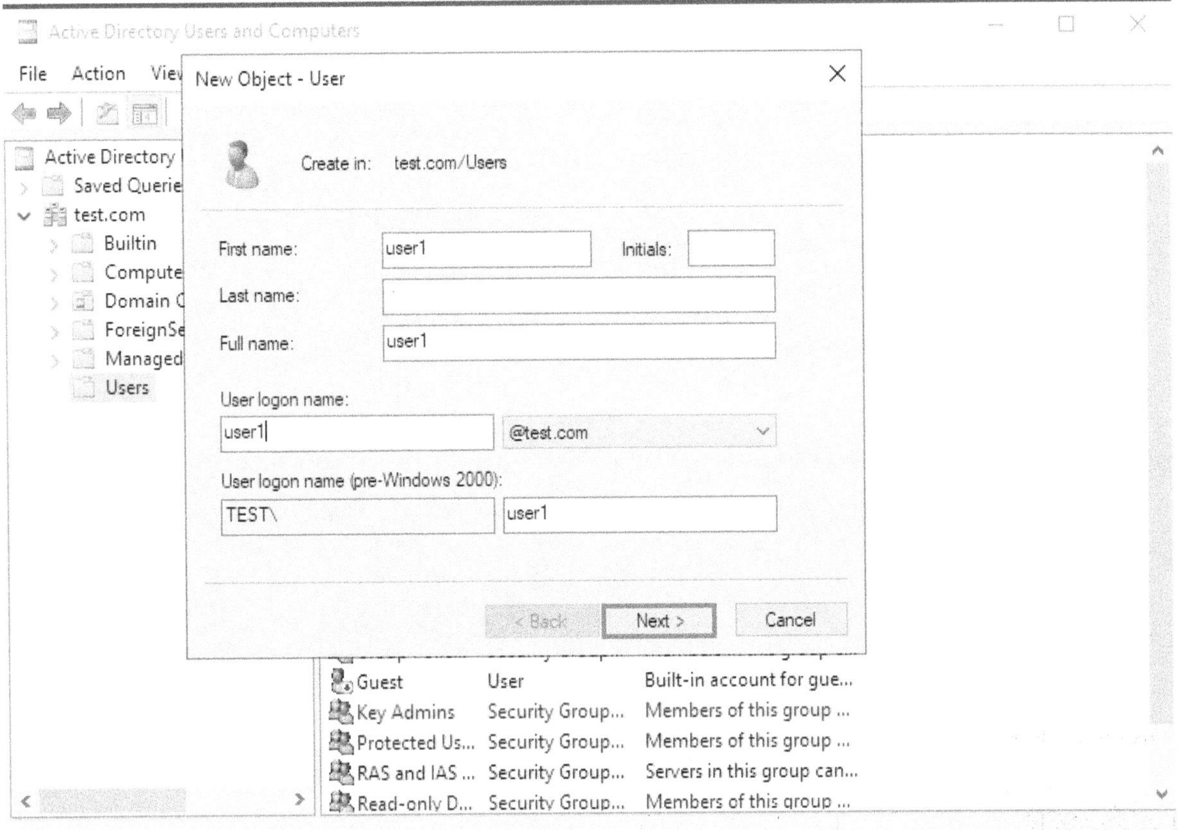

4. Set a password for a new User Click Next.

- Tick User cannot change password.
- Tick Password never expires.

If you need the user to change the password at the next logon Tick User must change password at the next logon.

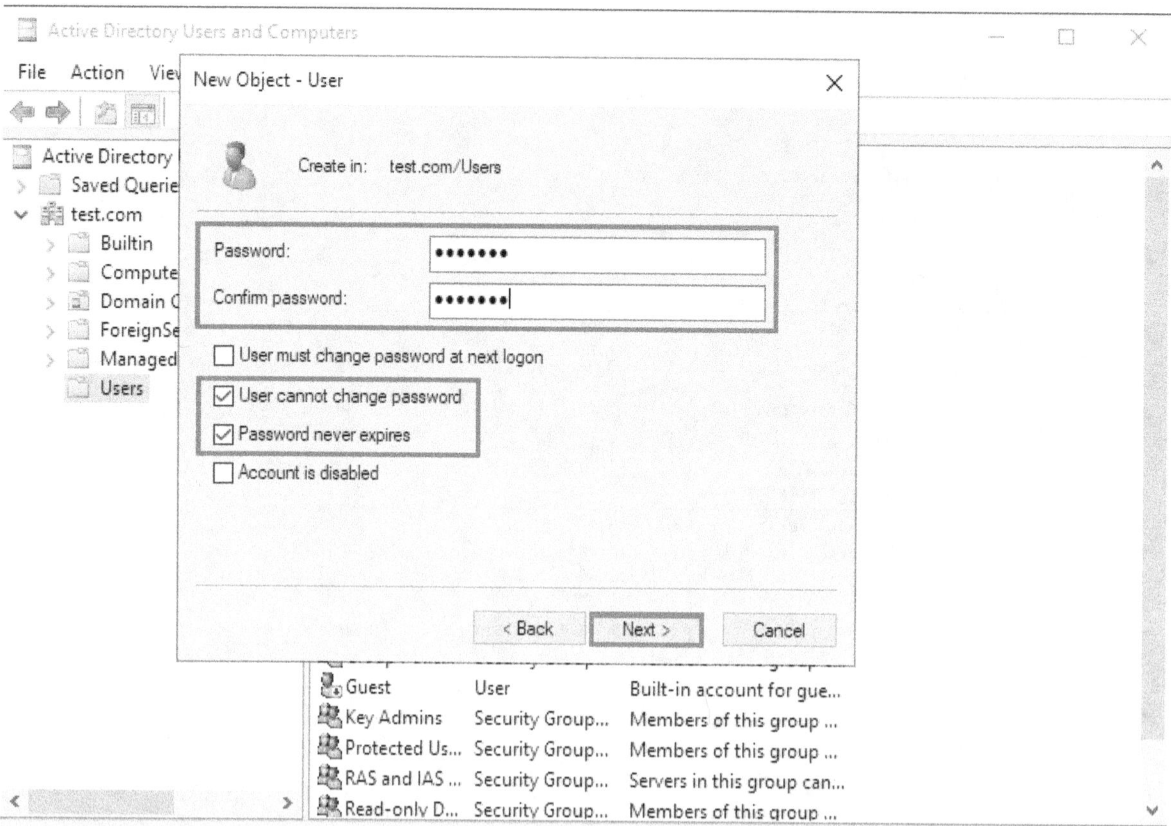

5. Click Finish.

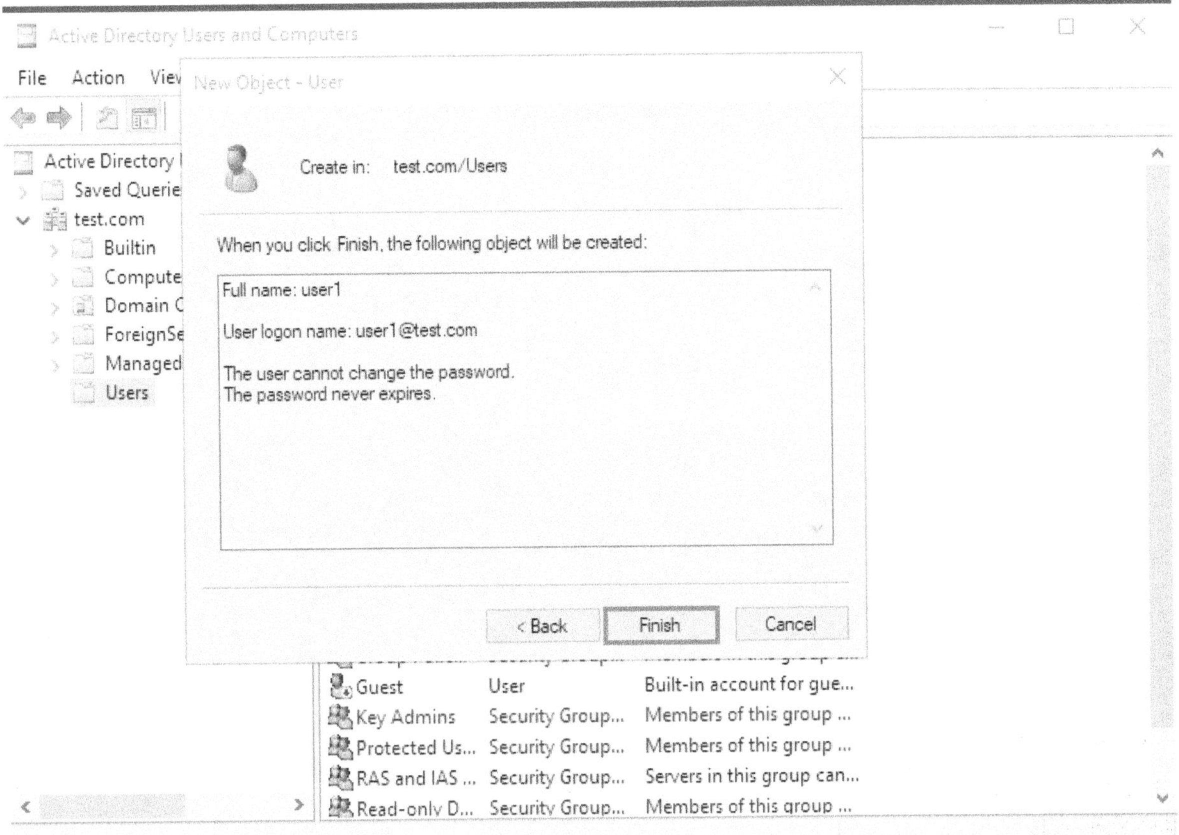

The Active Directory User has been created.

Create Group on Active Directory – Windows Server 2022

In this step, we are going to create a group and add users to the group.

1. Open Server Manager, click Tools and select Active Directory Users and Computer.

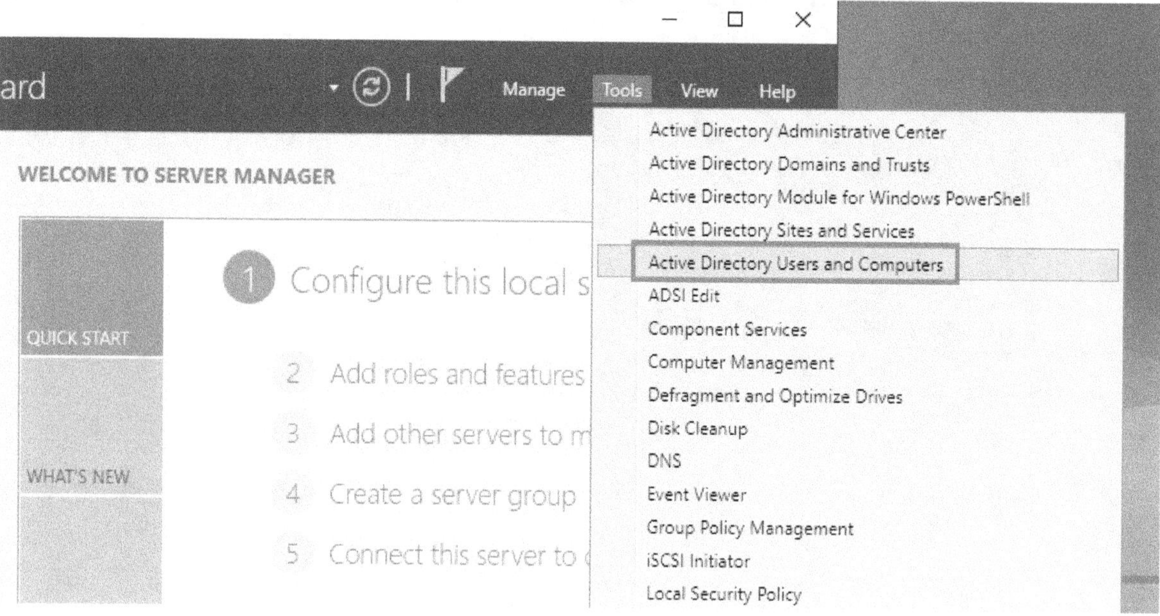

2. Right-click on Users, click New and select Group.

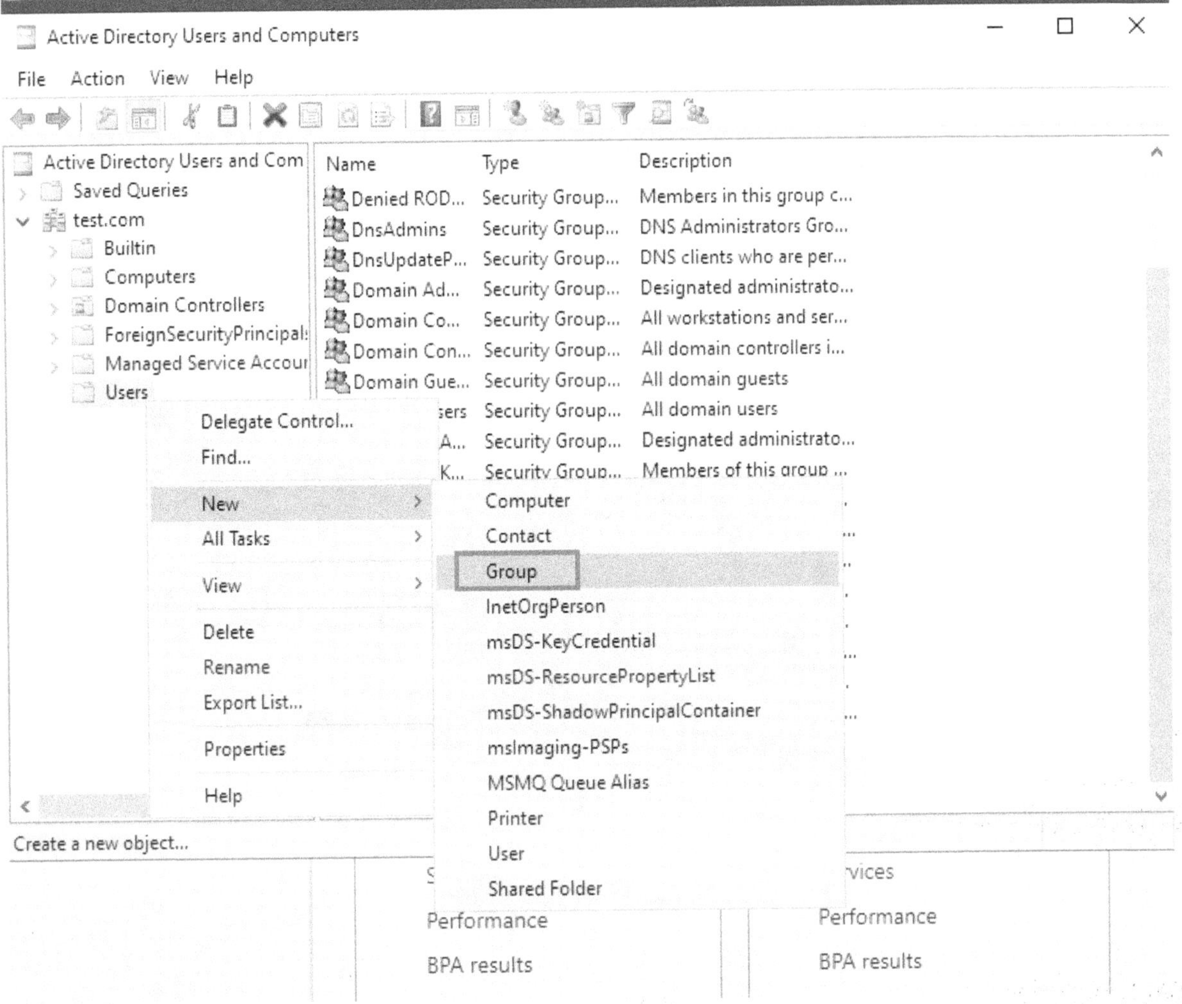

3. Enter the Group name and click OK.

- Default Group scope: Global
- Default Group type: Security

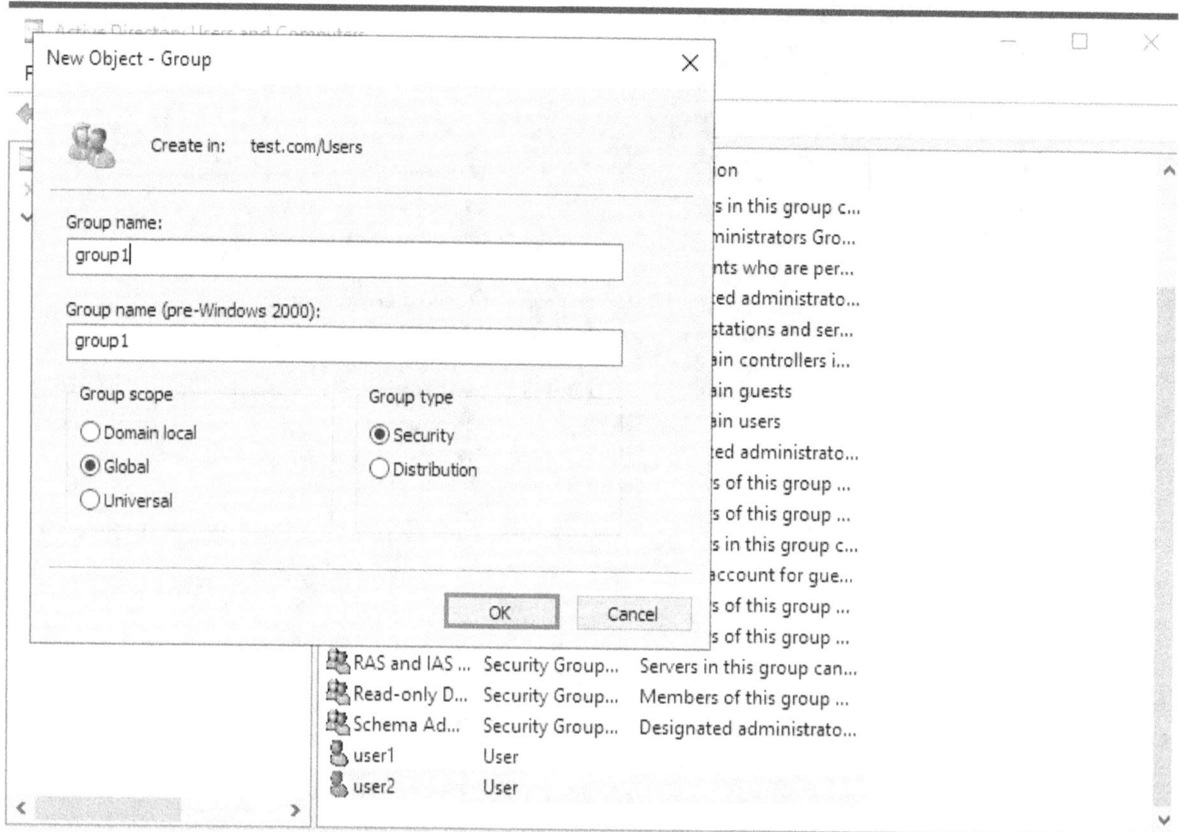

4. Right-click on the Group name and select Properties.

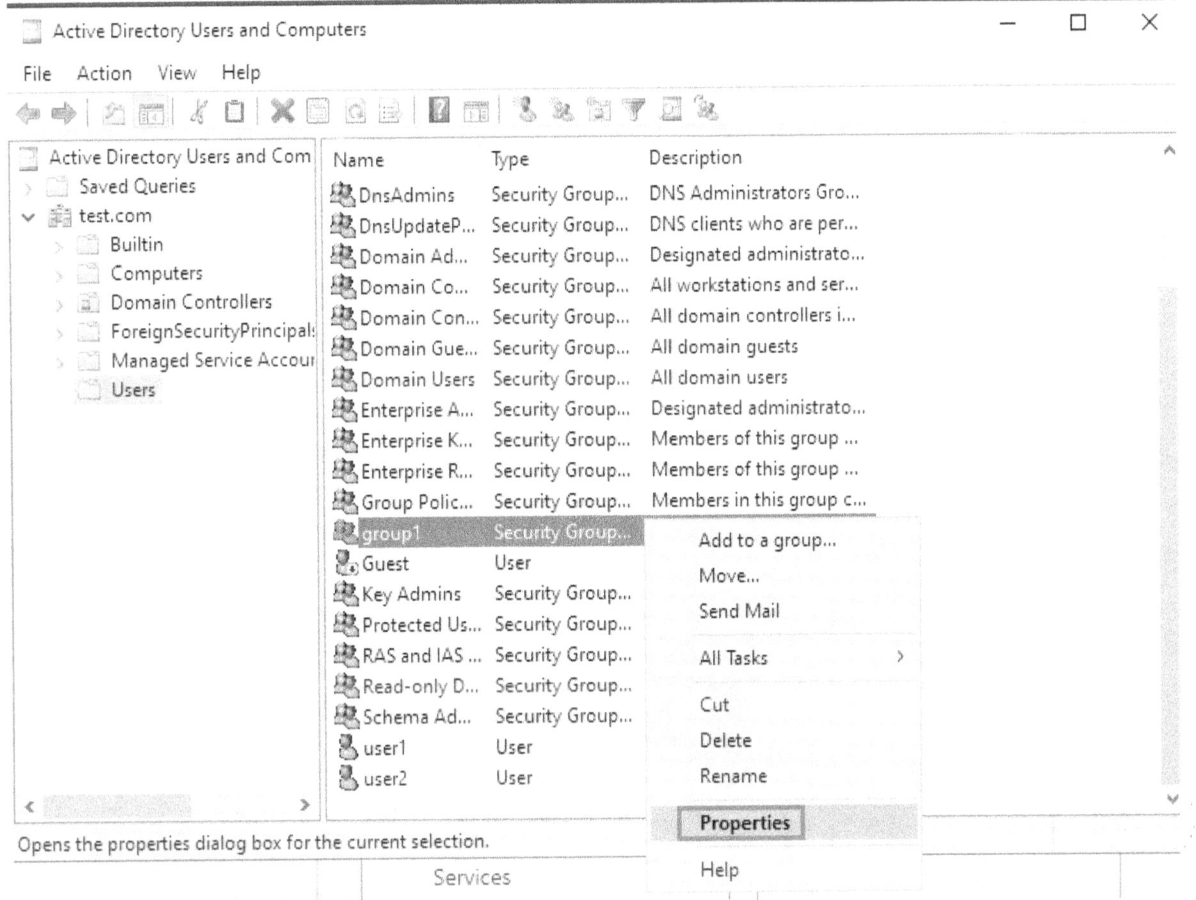

5. Select the Members tab and click Add.

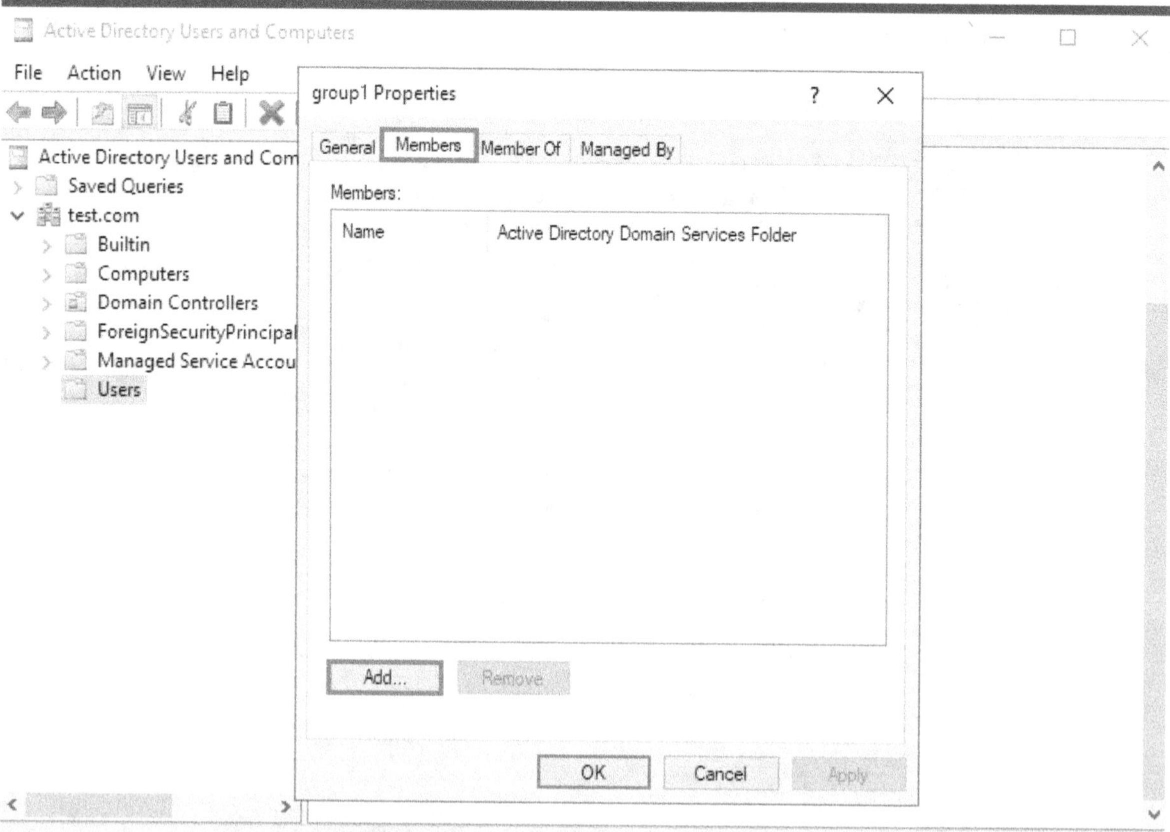

6. Click Advanced.

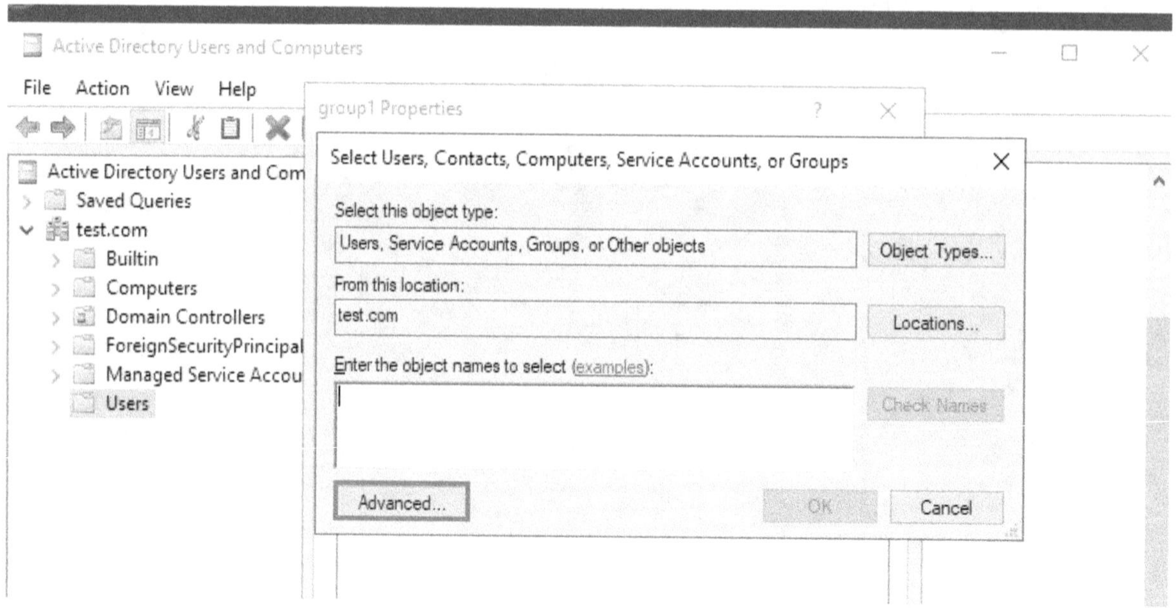

7. Click Find Now, Select the Users and Click OK.

In this tutorial, we select user1 and user2.

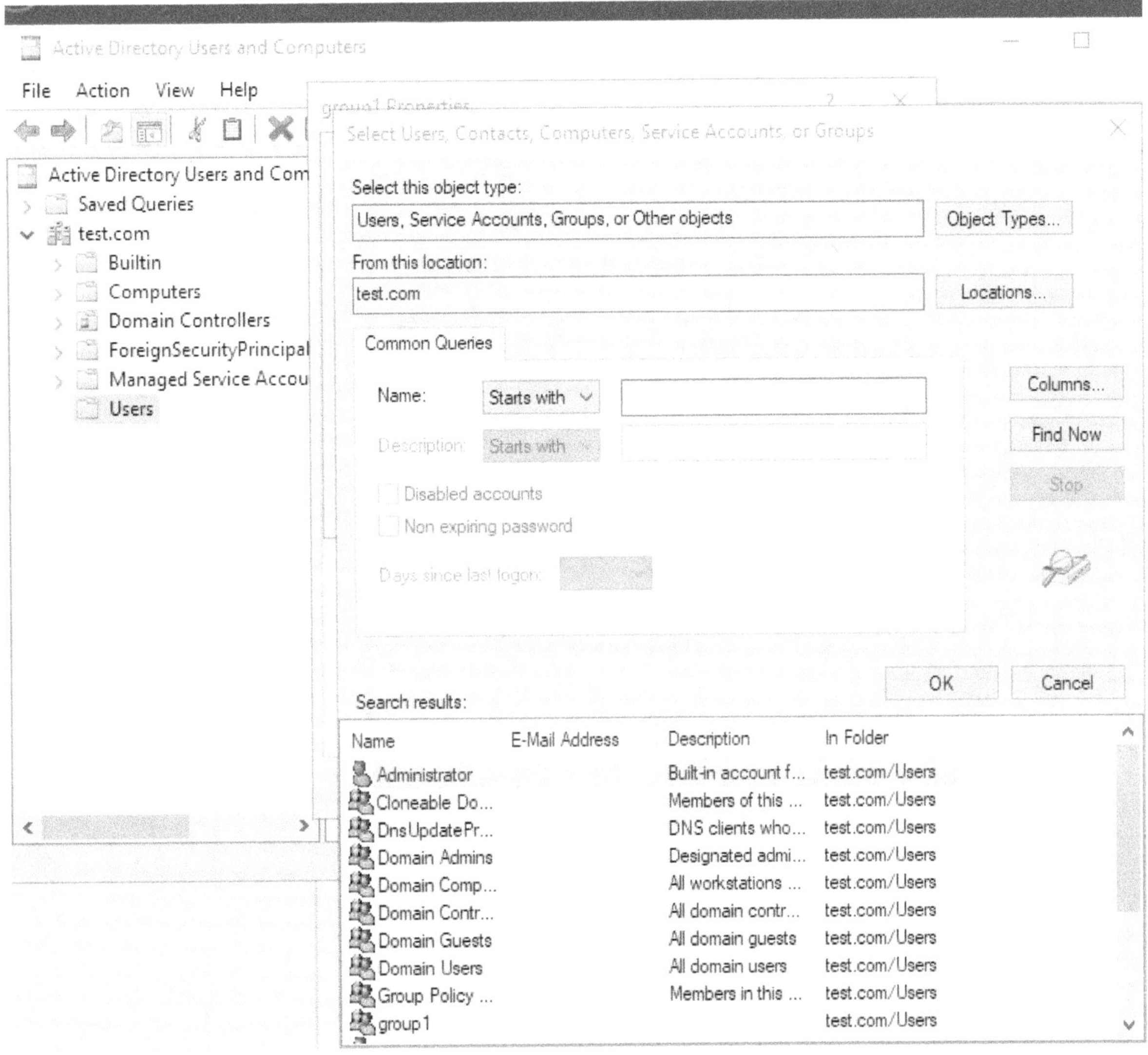

8. Click OK.

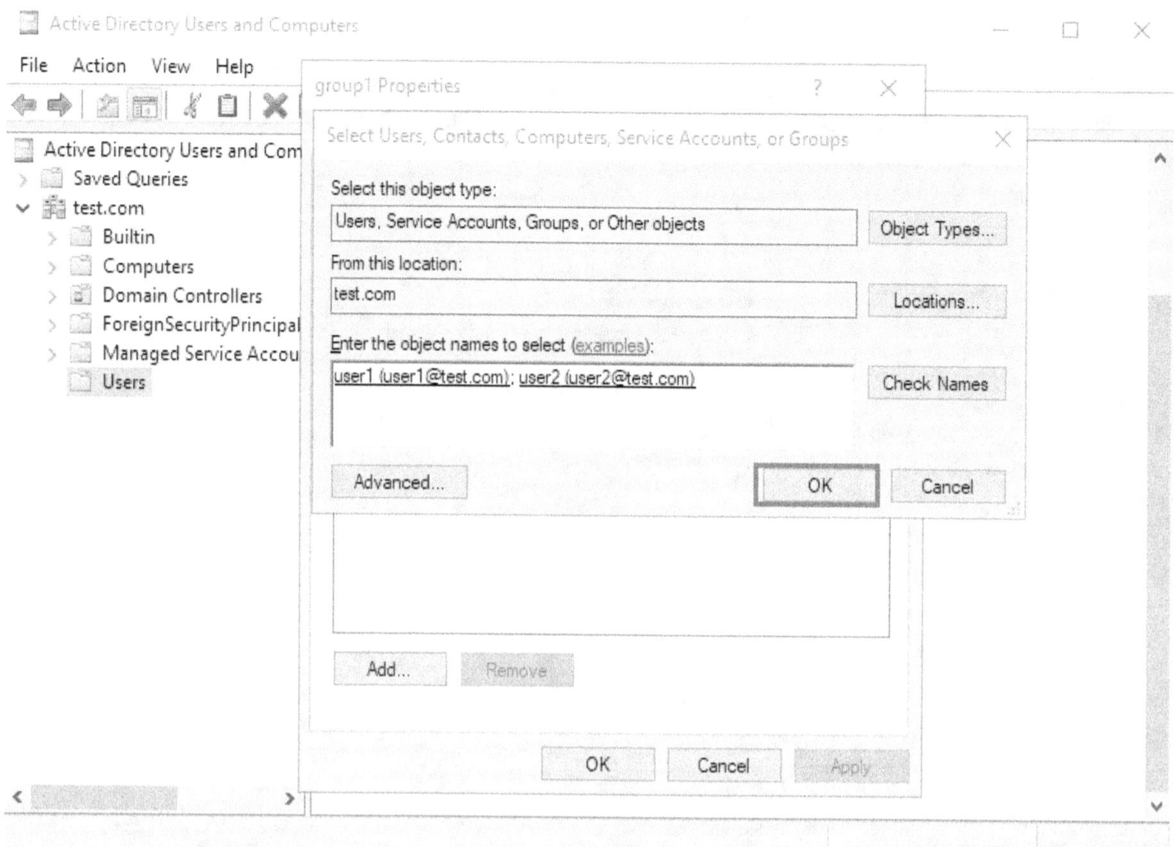

9. Click OK.

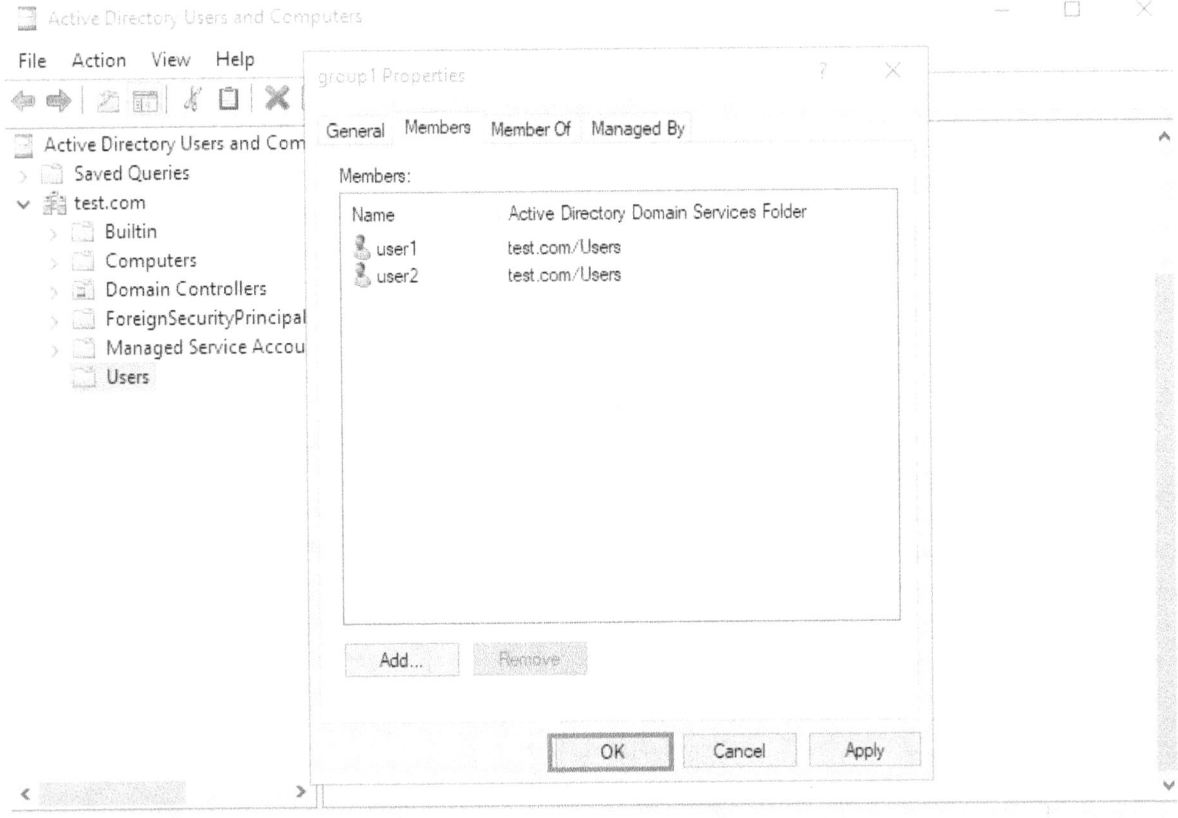

The Active Directory Group has been created.

Delete or remove a user from Active Directory

Use the following steps to delete a new user from Active Directory:

1. Log in to your domain controller by using Remote Desktop.

2. Use one of the following options to open **Active Directory Users and Computers**:

   - Right-click the **Start** menu, select **Run**, enter **dsa.msc**, and click **OK**.

   - Use the Windows search function by clicking on **Start** and entering **dsa.msc**.

- Click on **Server Manager -> Tools** and select **Active Directory Users and Computers** from the menu.

3. Expand your domain from the left-hand menu.

4. To use the **Find** function in Active Directory, right-click your domain and select **Find**. Ensure
that you select **Users, Contacts, and Groups** from the **Find** drop-down menu. Then, type the **Name**
of the user you want to delete.

5. You can delete or disable the user.
   Note: Deleting the user is not reversible.

   - To delete the user, right-click the user and select **delete**.
     Click **Yes** in the confirmation
     window if you are sure.

   - To disable the user, right-click the user and select **disable**.
     Click **Yes** in the confirmation
     window if you are sure.

Create a new group within Active Directory

Use the following steps to create a new group in Active Directory:

1. Log in to your domain controller by using the Remote Desktop.

2. Use one of the following options to open **Active Directory Users and Computers**:

   - Right-click the **Start** menu, select **Run**, enter **dsa.msc**, and click **OK**.

   - Use the Windows search function by clicking on **Start** and entering **dsa.msc**.

- Click on **Server Manager -> Tools** and select **Active Directory Users and Computers** from the menu.

3. Expand your domain from the left-hand menu.

4. Depending on whether you are using organizational units or not, find the appropriate object to place
the user in. By default, the built-in Microsoft default groups are under the **Users** organization unit.
If you prefer, you can put the user in a custom organization unit.

5. Right-click the object you want to choose for the user, select **New**, and select **Group**.

6. In the wizard, enter your group name. By default, the wizard preselects **Global** under **Group Scope**
and **Security** under **Group Type**. Do not change the group type to **Distribution** because that option
creates distribution groups for Microsoft Exchange® and e-mail.

Add or remove users to or from a group

You can add and remove a user to or from a group from the **Group** or from the **User**. This section describes
both options.

Use the following steps to add or remove a users to or from groups in Active Directory:

1. Log in to your domain controller by using Remote Desktop.

2. Use one of the following options to open **Active Directory Users and Computers**:

   - Right-click the **Start** menu, select **Run**, enter **dsa.msc**, and click **OK**.

- o Use the Windows search function by clicking on **Start** and entering **dsa.msc**.

- o Click on **Server Manager -> Tools** and select **Active Directory Users and Computers** from the menu.

3. Expand your domain from the left-hand menu.

4. To add the user to a group from the **Group**, use the following steps:

   a. Right-click your domain and select **Find**. Ensure that you select **Users, Contacts, and Groups** from the **Find** drop-down menu. Enter the **Name** of the group and click **Find Now**.

   b. Right-click the group and select **Properties**.

   c. Click the **Members** tab.

   d. To remove a user, click the user to highlight it and click **Remove**.

   e. To add a user, click **Add**. Type the username into **Enter the object names to select**. Click **Check Names**. Click **OK** when the wizard underlines the name.

5. To add a user to a group from the **User**, use the following steps:

   a. Right-click your domain and select **Find**. Ensure that you select **Users, Contacts, and Groups** from the **Find** drop-down menu. Enter the **Name** of the user and click **Find Now**.

   b. Right-click the user and select **Properties**.

   c. Click the **Member Of** tab.

d. To remove the user from a group, click the group and
click **Remove**.

e. To add the user to a group click **Add**. Type the group name into
Enter the object names to select. Click **Check Names** and
click **OK** when the wizard underlines the name.

Delete a Group within Active Directory

Use the following steps to delete a group from Active Directory:

1. Log in to your domain controller by using Remote Desktop.

2. Use one of the following options to open **Active Directory Users and Computers**:

     o Right-click the **Start** menu, select **Run**, enter **dsa.msc**, and click **OK**.

     o Use the Windows search function by clicking on **Start** and entering **dsa.msc**.

     o Click on **Server Manager -> Tools** and select **Active Directory Users and Computers** from the menu.

3. Expand your domain from the left-hand menu.

4. To use the **Find** function within Active Directory, right-click your domain and select **Find**. Ensure
that you select **Users, Contacts, and Groups** from the **Find** drop down menu. Type the **Name** of the
group you want to delete.

5. Right-click the group and select **delete**. Click **Yes** in the confirmation window if you are sure.

....

How to Join a Windows 11 PC to a Domain

A Windows 11 PC is designed for all kinds of environments. It can work perfectly fine as a stand-alone machine, but you can also manage it as part of a wider network.

If you're managing multiple devices on Windows 11, you'll probably want to join it to a domain. A domain facilitates the management and security of PCs from a single server (or several servers). You can then use a single user account to log in to multiple devices and access different server resources on any PC.

You don't need to be a network admin to do this, however. You might want to join your laptop to an office or educational domain—if you have permission to do so. If you're unsure how to join a Windows 11 PC to a domain, follow the steps we've outlined below.

Things You Need to Join a Windows 11 PC to a Domain

If you want to join a domain, the following is needed:

- A Windows 11 PC running **Windows 11 Professional, Enterprise,** or **Education.**
- A suitable account on an **Active Directory** domain (with a username and password).
- The device is on the same network (it works <u>over a VPN connection</u>) as the domain with access to the **domain controller.**

Joining a Windows 11 PC to a domain isn't an easy step for beginners, and we'll be using industry-specific terms in this article. If you're unsure, make sure to consult with a network administrator before you begin.

How to Join a Windows 11 PC to a Domain

If you think you're ready to join your Windows 11 PC to a domain, and you're on the same network, you can start now.

To join a Windows 11 PC to a domain:

1. Open the **Start** menu and press **Settings.**
2. In Settings, press **Accounts > Access work or school** and click on the **Connect** button.

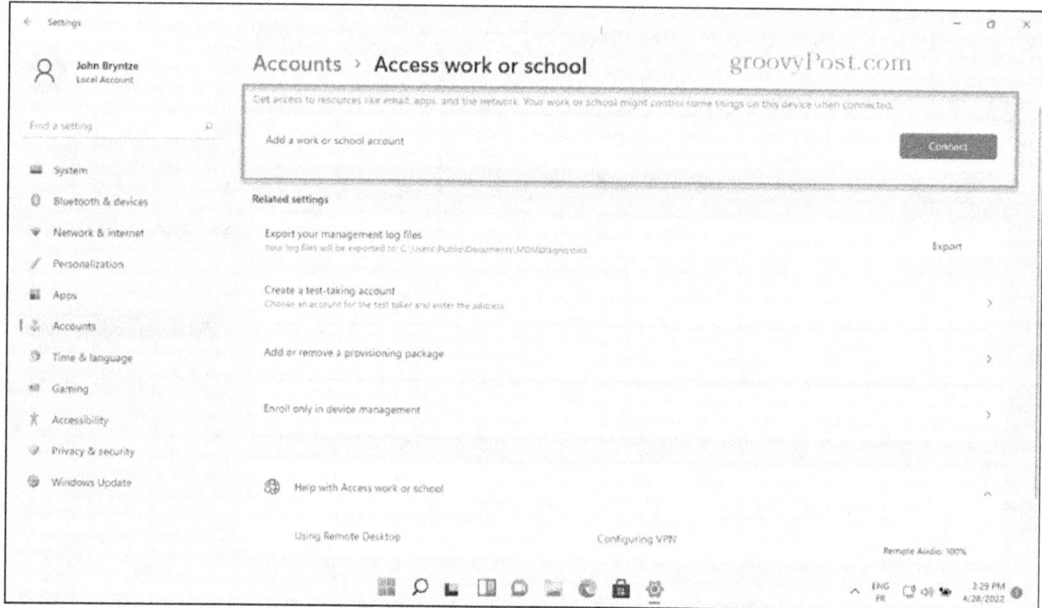

3. Select the **Join this device to a local Active Directory domain** option.

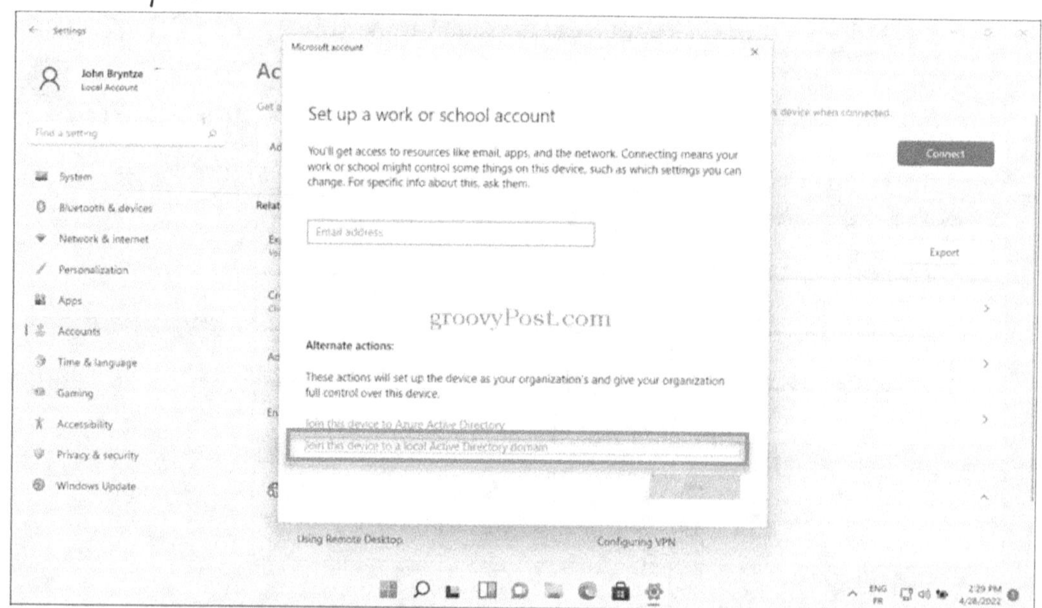

4. Type in the **domain name** when instructed.

- There are two different types of domain name we can use here. We use the **single legacy name** or the more **extended name** separated with dots, similar to a web address. In our image below, the legacy domain name is 'bryntze', and the longer so-called DNS (also called FQDN) domain name is 'ad.bryntze.cloud'. You can use either name given by your network administrator.

5. Joining the device to the domain requires the correct permissions. If your network administrator has given your account access, you can enter your credentials. If not, ask your network administrator to enter their admin credentials to join the device for you.

6. We might see an extra dialog to **Add an account**. However, this isn't necessary to join the device to the domain, so press the **Skip** button.

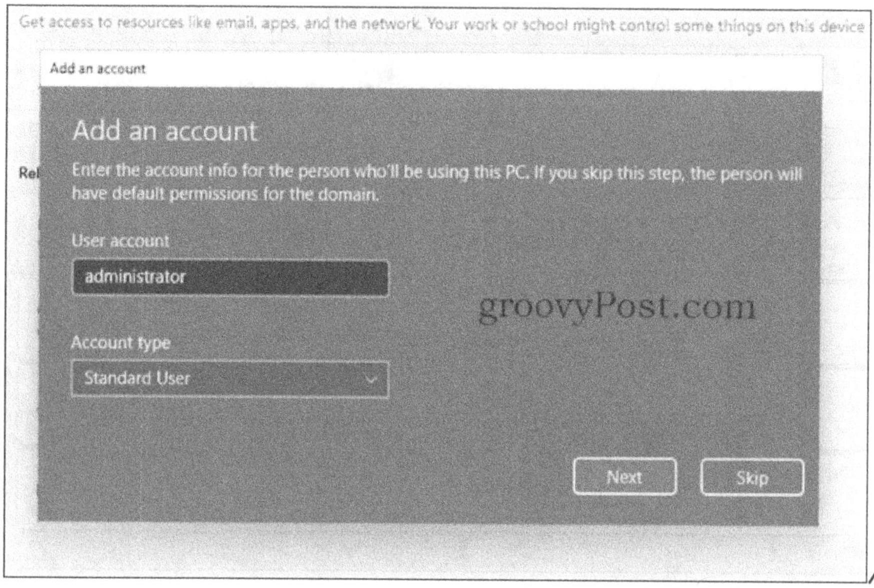

7. At this point, your account should be set up in Active Directory. You'll need to _restart your PC_ when prompted to do so.

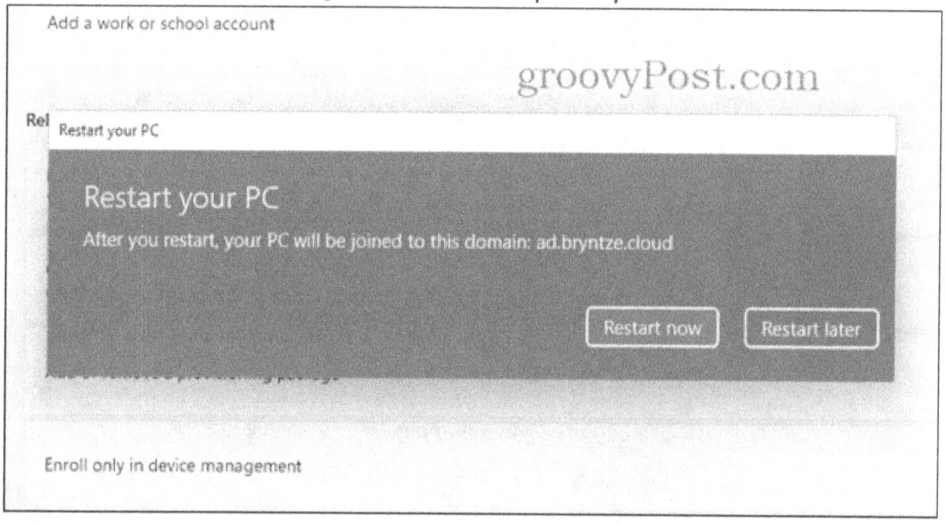

8. After restarting the Windows 11 device, we can now log in with our domain user. To do this, type

in **DOMAIN\username** or the **User Principle Name** (often the same as our email address).

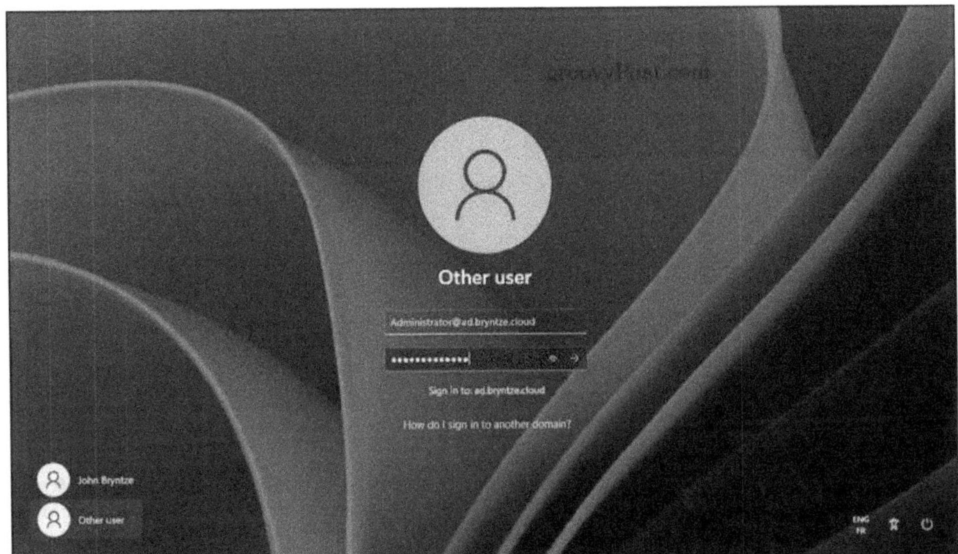

9. Once you've logged in, we can go to **Settings > Accounts > Access work or school** again and verify that our domain shows up.

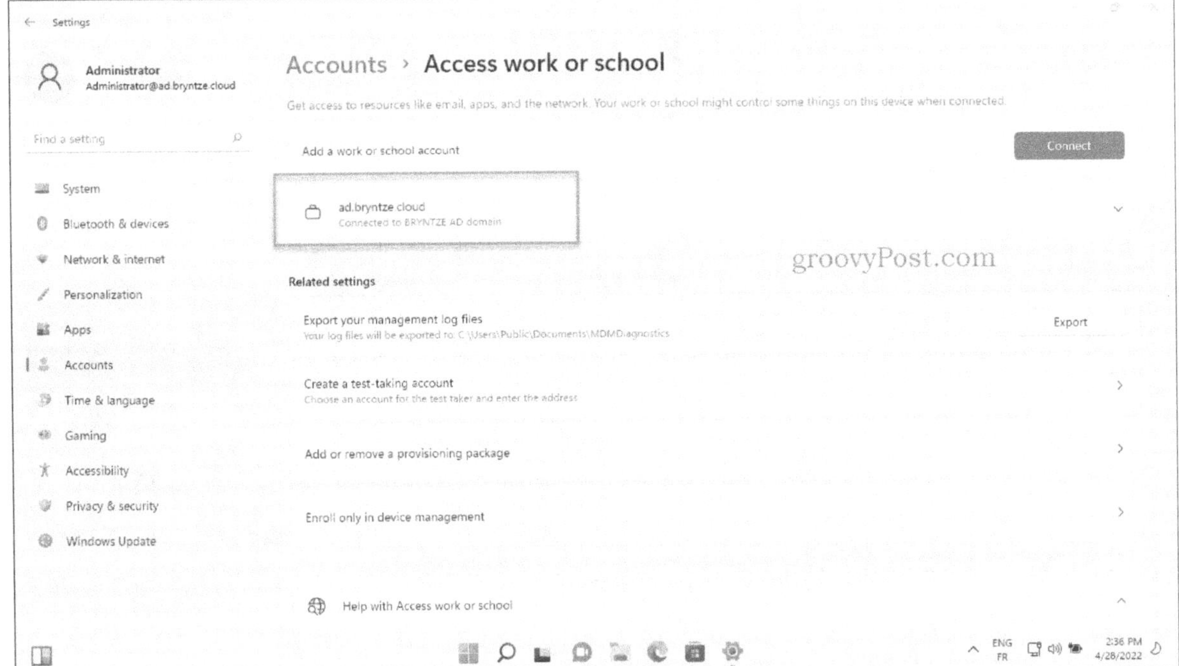

How to Leave a Domain on Windows 11

If you want to remove a PC from a local domain, you can do so from **Settings**. However, before you do this, make sure that you have a **local or Microsoft account** with access to your PC on the device already.

If you don't, you may lock yourself out of your PC once you remove it from the domain. If you have administrator access over your PC, you can set up a new local user account before you follow these steps. You can also enable the built-in administrator account instead.

To leave a domain on Windows 11:

1. Open the **Start** menu and press **Settings**.
2. In **Settings**, press **Accounts > Access work or school**.
3. Click on the little arrow down right to the domain name, then press the **Disconnect** button.

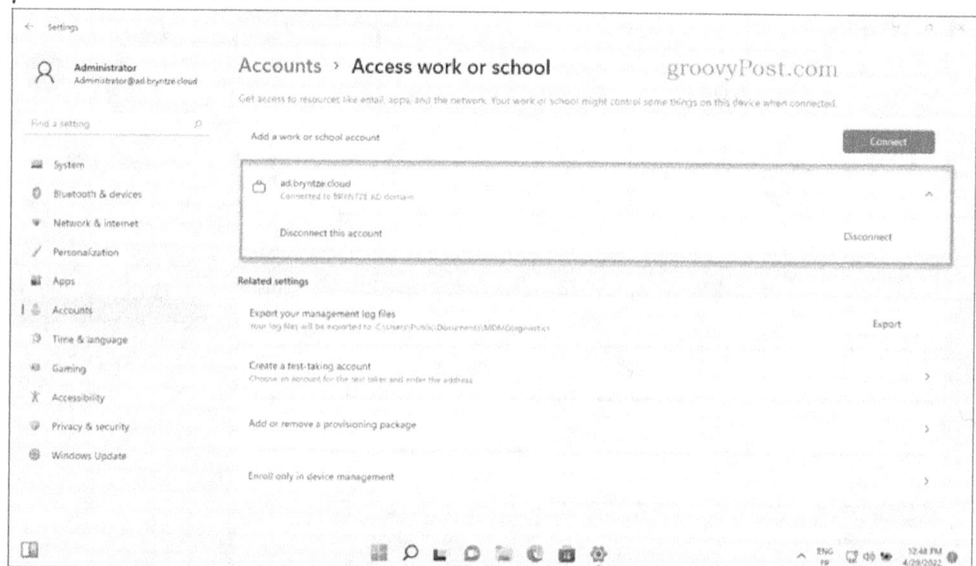

4. You'll need to confirm you want to leave the domain. Follow the steps to do this by pressing **Yes > Disconnect** or cancel the process by pressing **Cancel**.
5. Follow any other additional steps (when prompted) to complete the process, then restart your PC.

Once you've restarted, your PC will be back in Workgroup mode. You'll lose shared access to domain resources, and you won't be able to use the same login details on your PC.

Using a Windows 11 PC on a Domain

If you've followed the steps above, you should be to join a Windows 11 PC to a domain in just a few minutes. If you need to remove the device, you can quickly disconnect it via Settings. You can reconnect the device at any time, but only if the network administrator allows you to do so.

How to Join a Windows 10 PC to a Domain

A Domain-based network provides centralized administration of an entire network from a single computer called a server. Domains provide single user log on from any networked computer within the network perimeter. Users can access resources for which they have appropriate permission. While I do not want to go into the complexities of Domain networks, you can find out more by contacting your Network Administrator if you have difficulties connecting to your workplace domain.

To join a Domain, you must first ensure you have the following information and resources:

- A user account on the Domain, this information you can get from your Network Administrator.
- Name of Domain.
- A computer running Windows 10 Pro or Enterprise/Education editions
- Domain Controller must be running Windows Server 2003 (functional level or later).

- *I discovered during testing that Windows 10 does not support Windows 2000 Server Domain Controllers.*

Join a Windows 10 PC or Device to a Domain

On the Windows 10 PC, go to **Settings** > **System** > **About**, then click Join a domain.

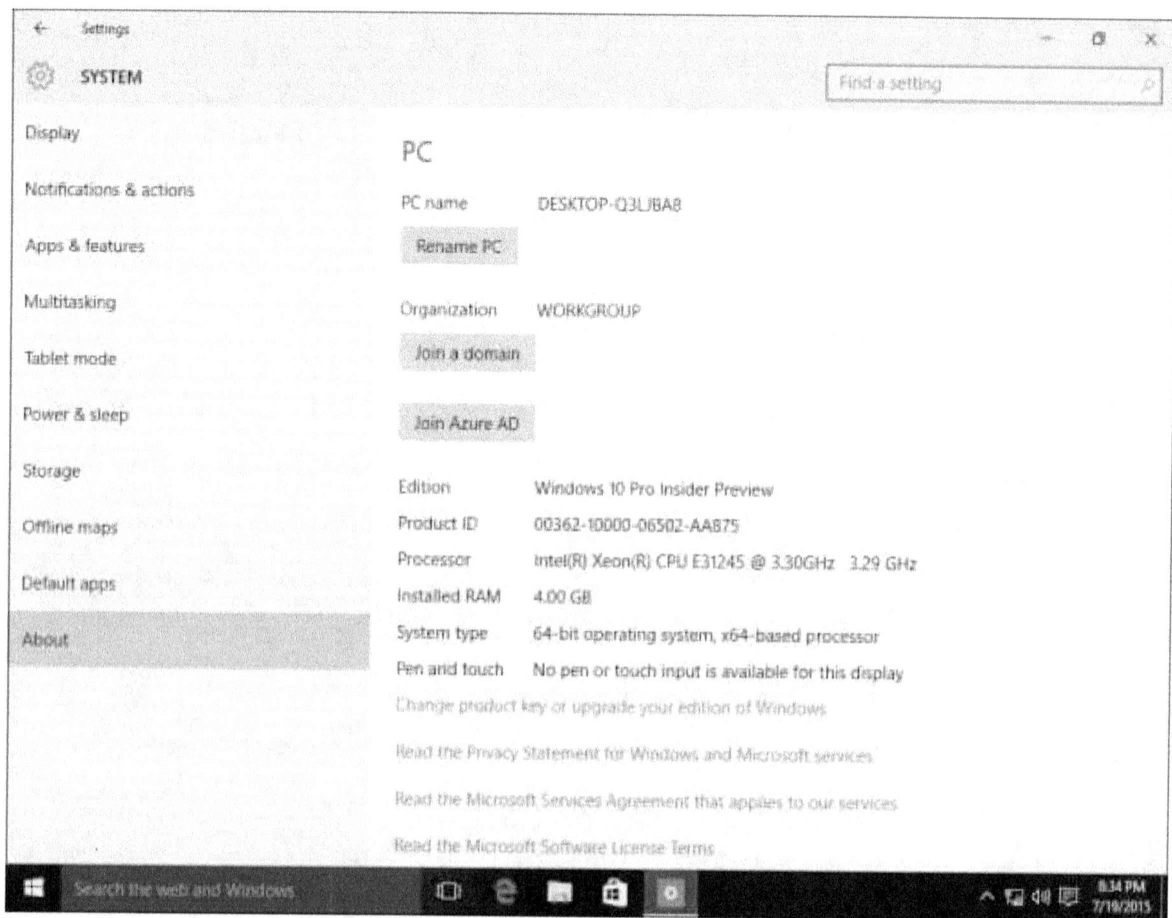

Enter the Domain name and click Next. You should have the correct domain info, but if not, contact your Network Administrator.

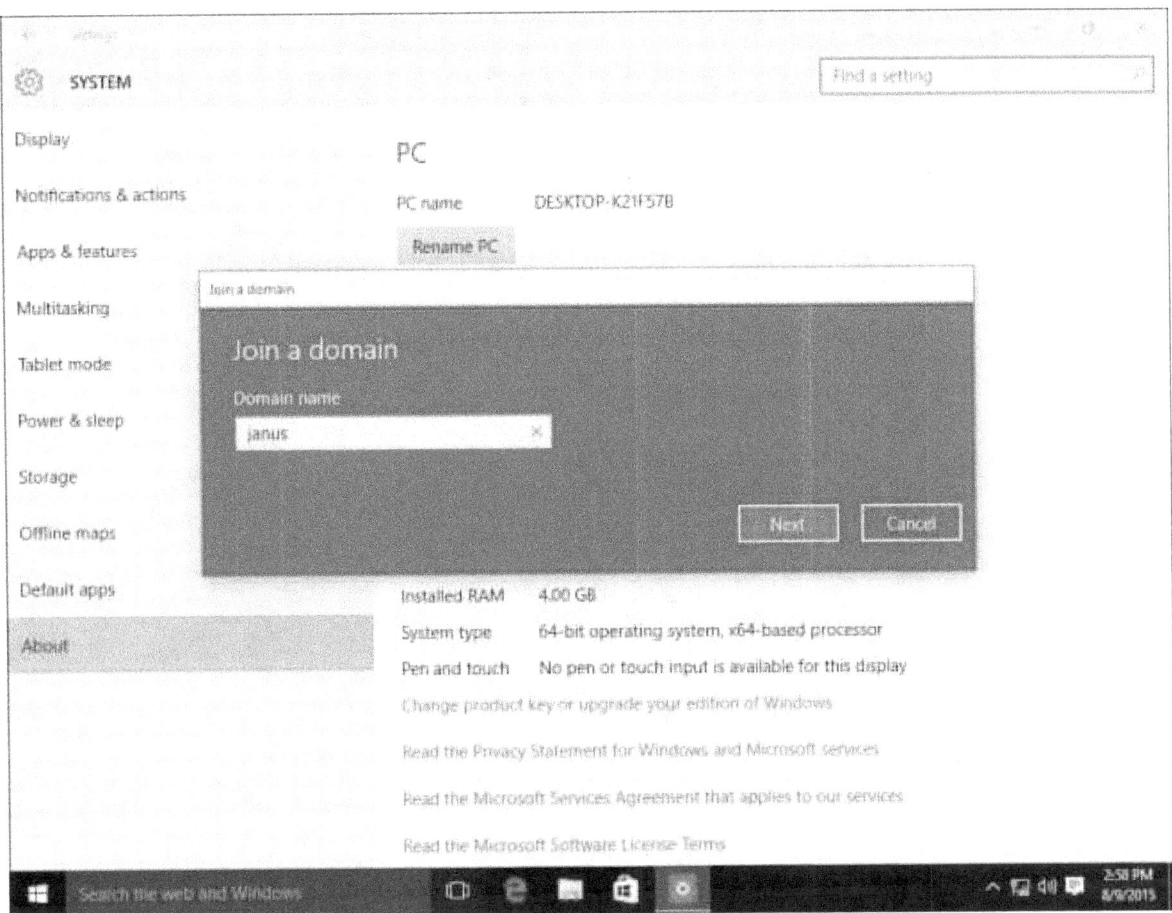

Enter account information that is used to authenticate on the Domain and then click OK.

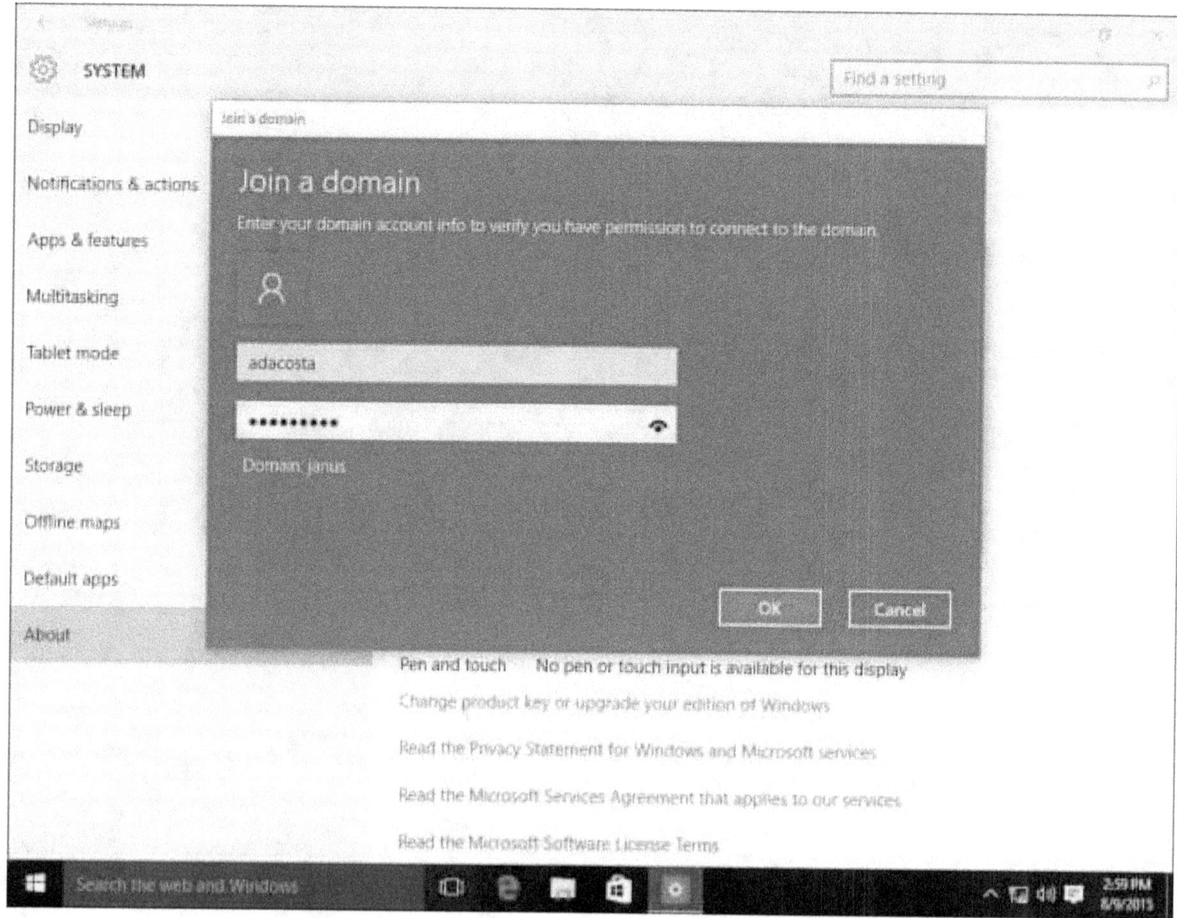

Wait while your computer is authenticated on the Domain.

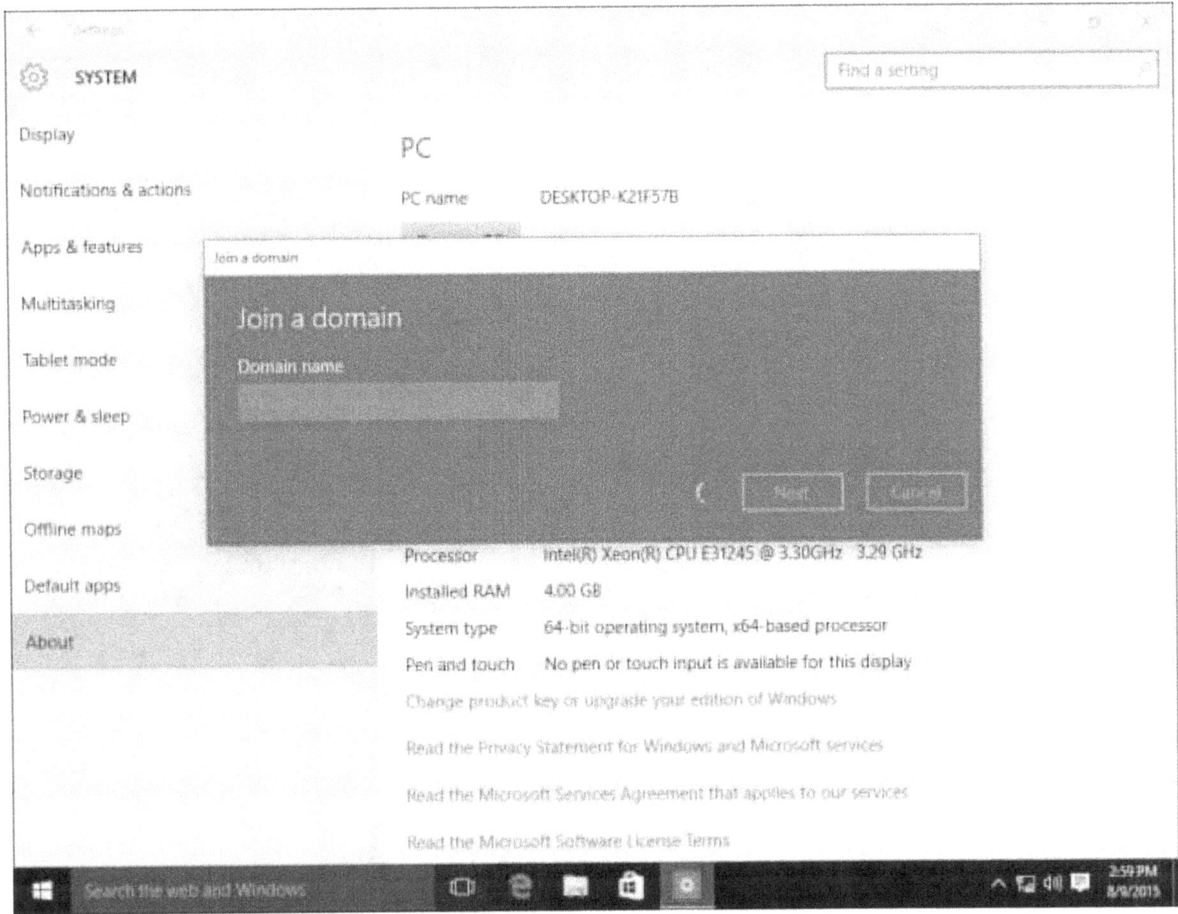

Click Next when you see this screen.

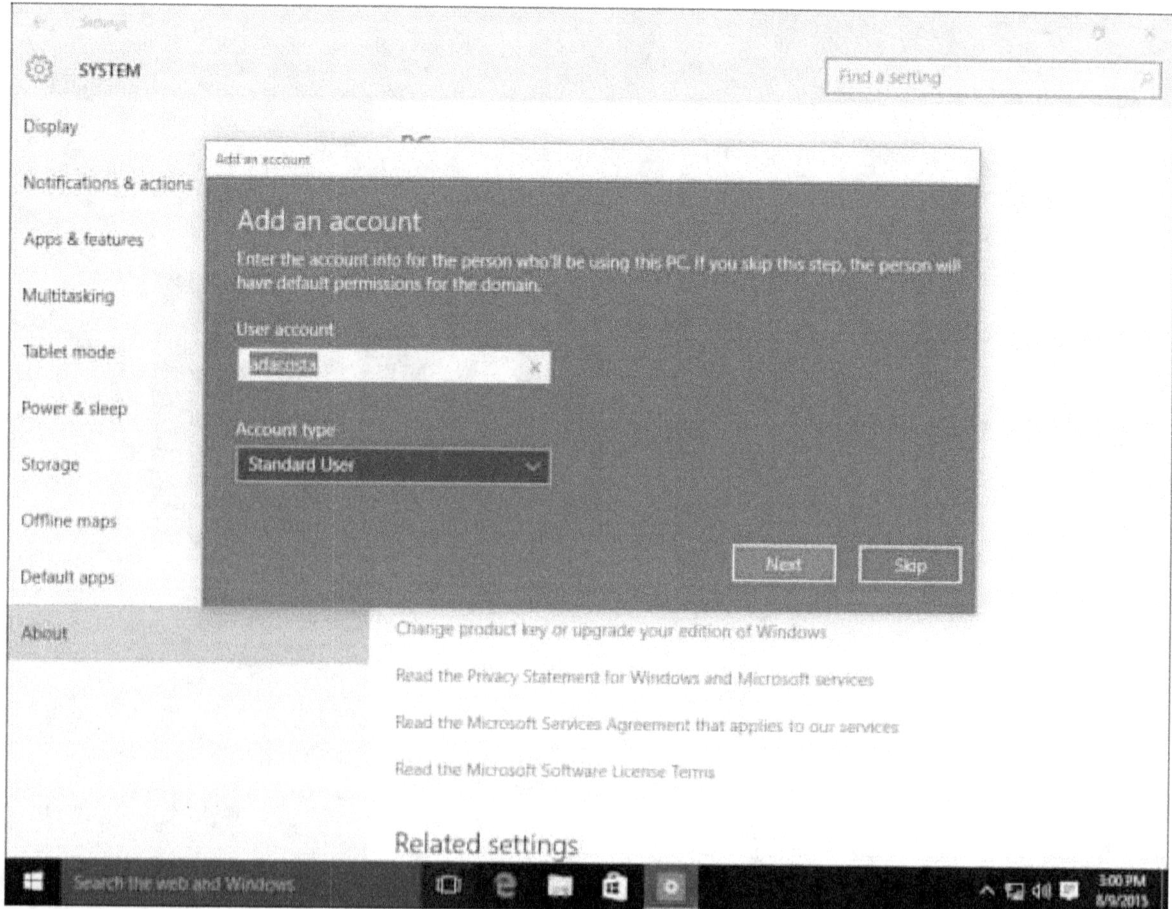

And then, you'll need to restart to complete the process.

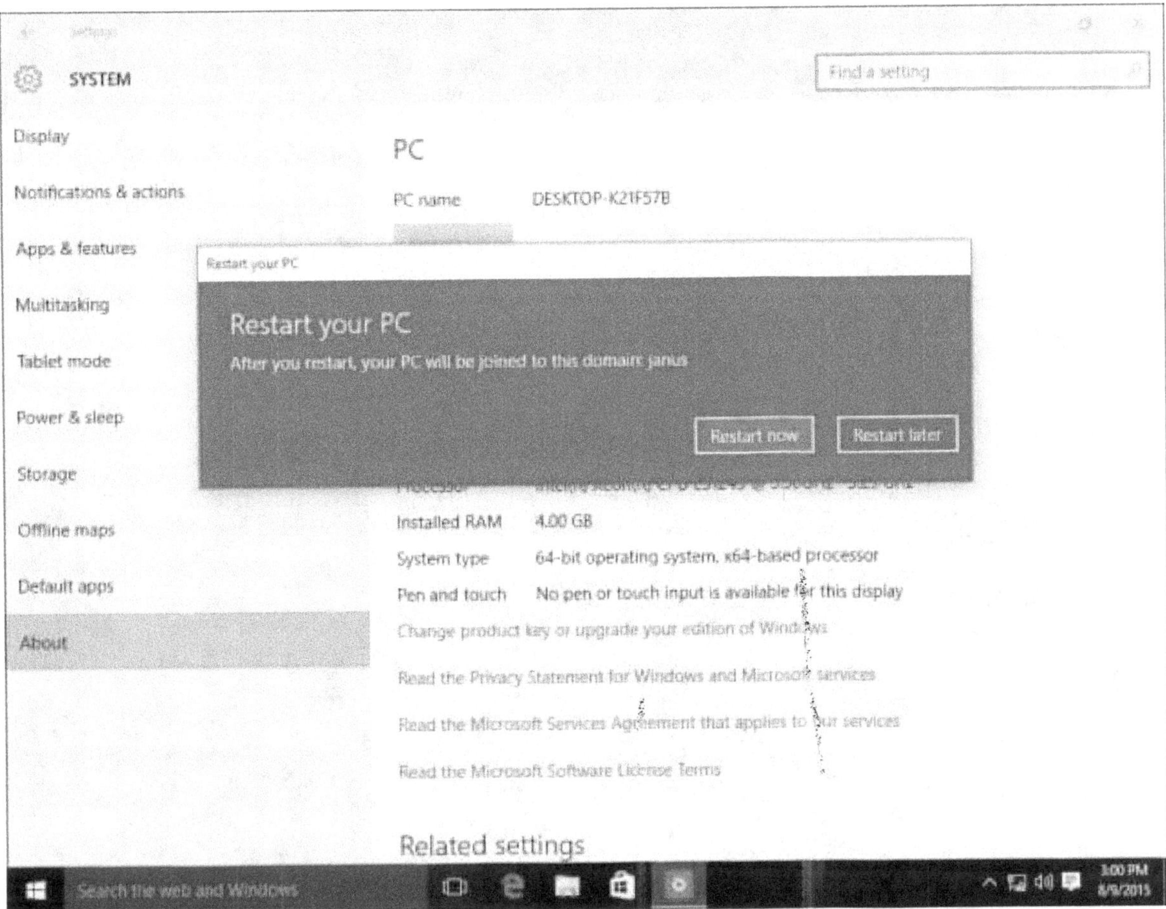

When the sign-in screen appears, you will notice the DOMAIN\User account is displayed. Enter your password, and you will now be logged onto your Domain.

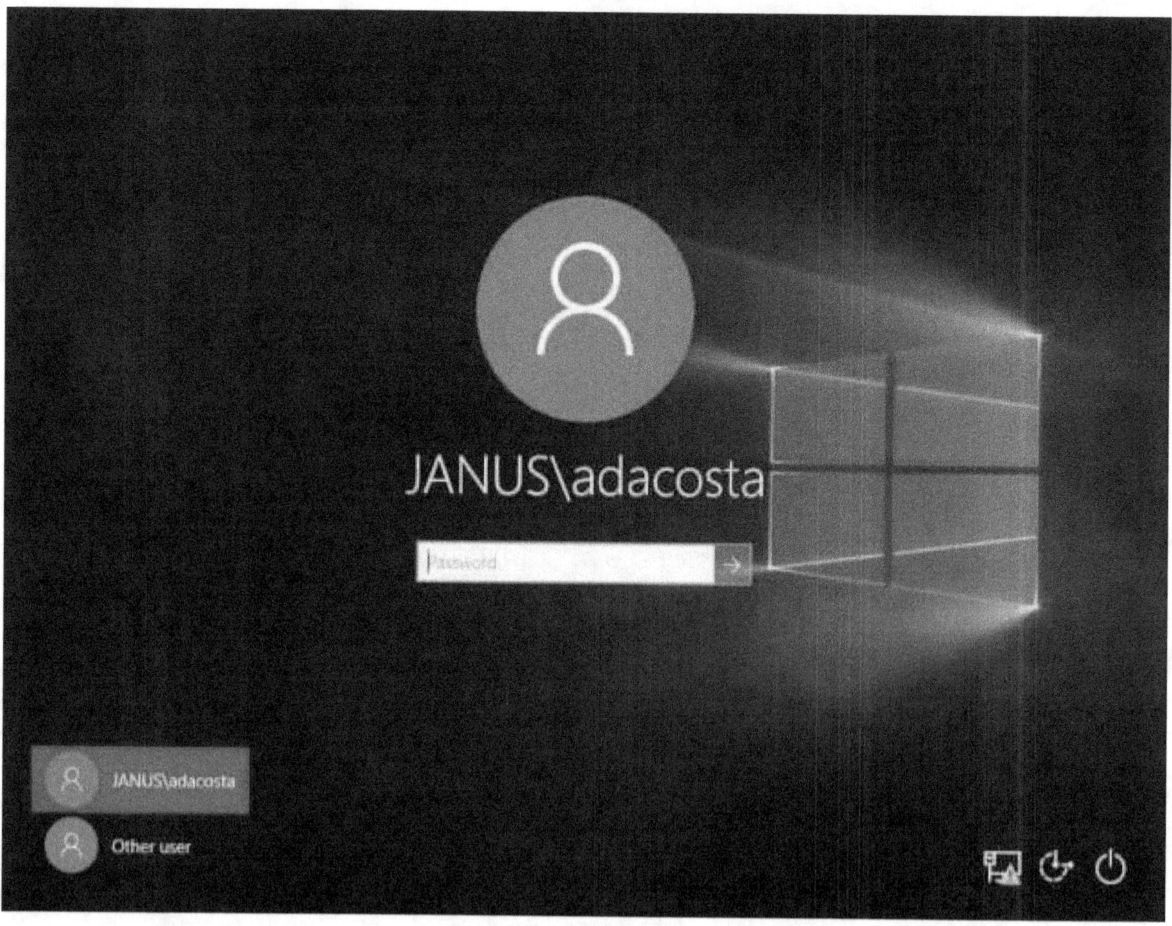

You will notice that once you are connected to the Domain, your About setting no longer lists options presented before. This is because the server centrally manages your computer.

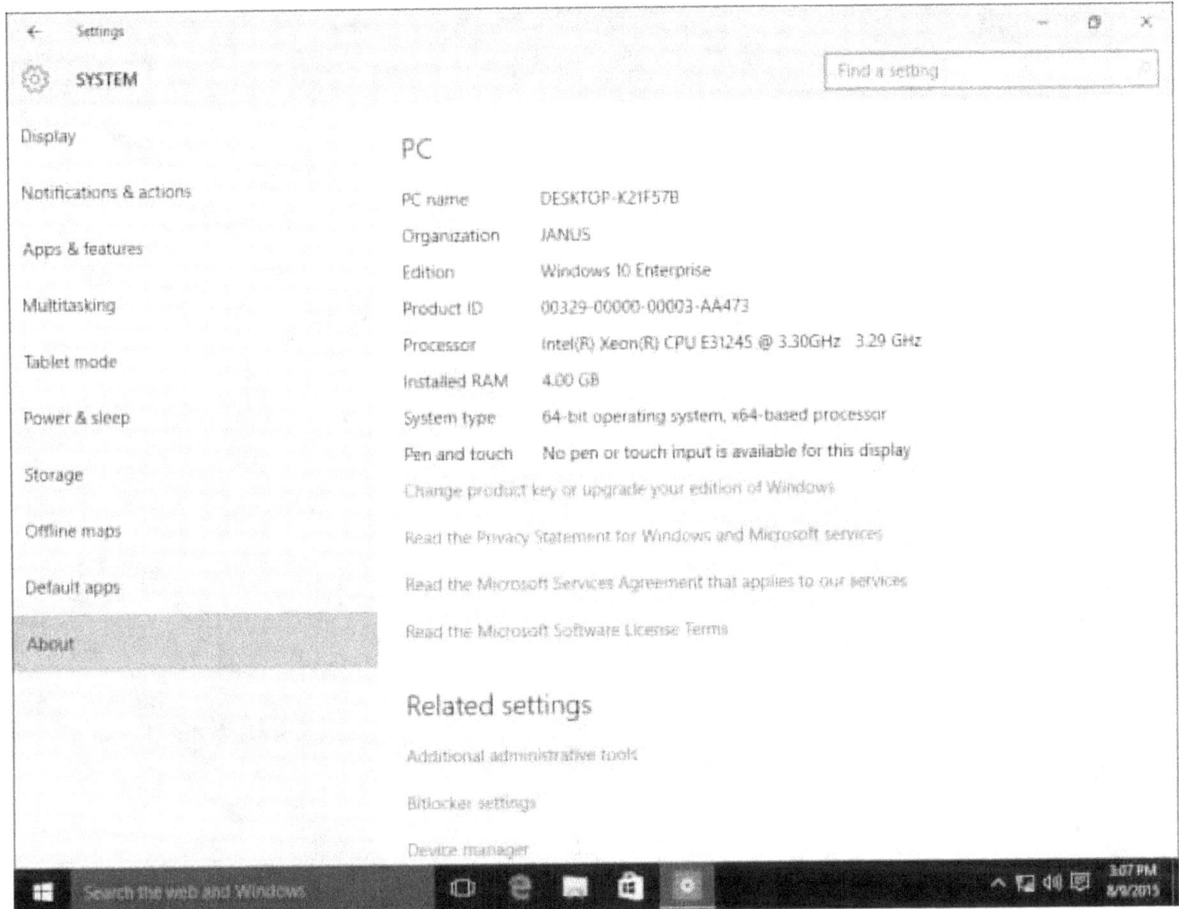

Leaving the Domain or log into your local account

If a need arises where you need to leave the domain or log into your local account, you can easily do so. Log into your local account while your computer is joined to a Domain. Sign out of your machine at the sign-in screen, select "Other" user.

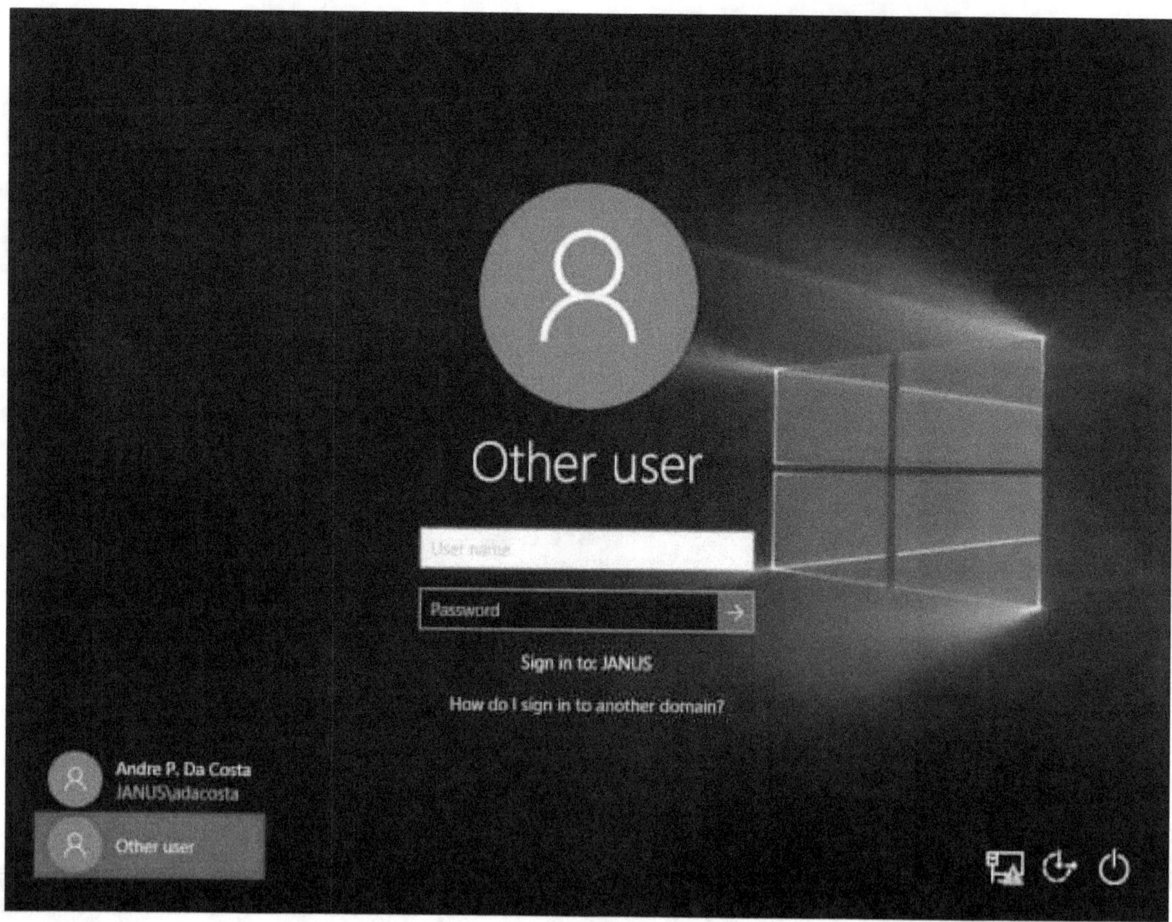

Enter the machine name followed by a backslash and then your local user account, as shown below.

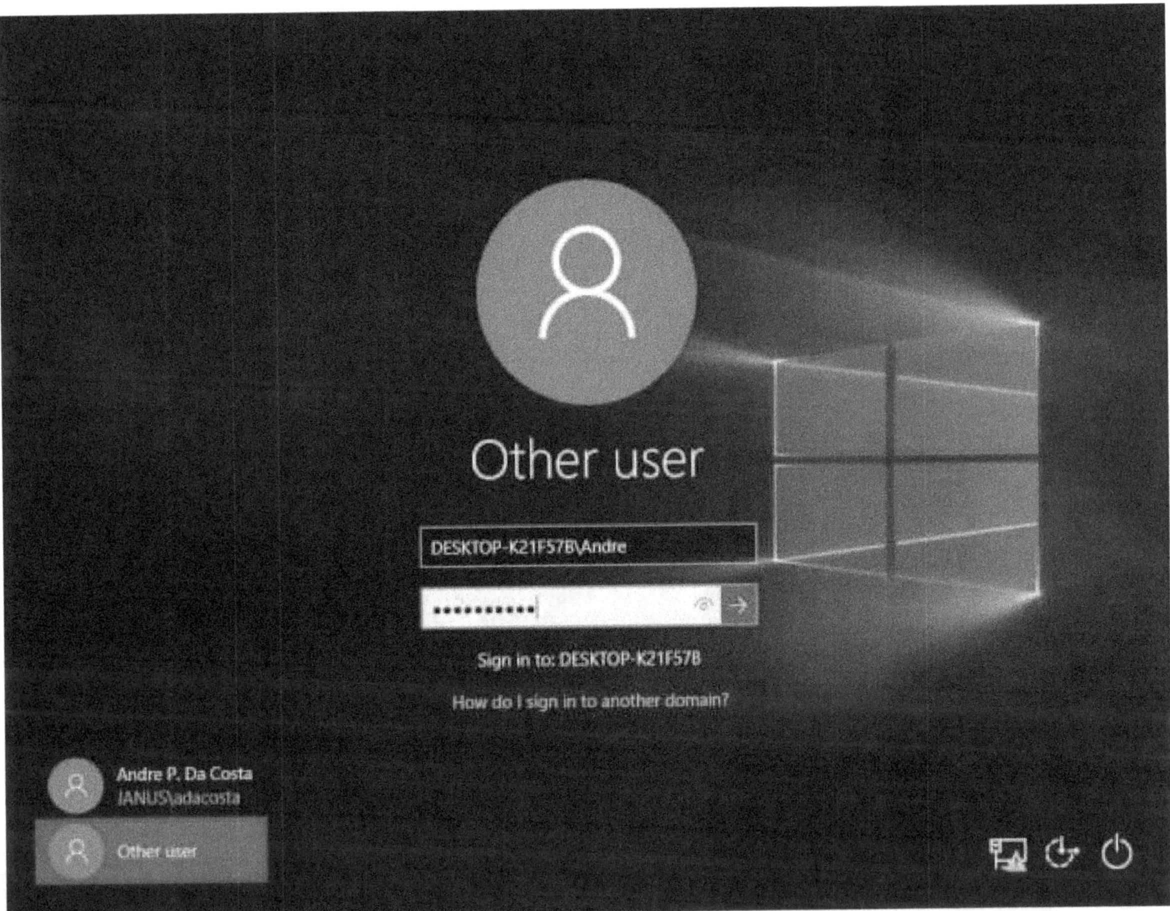

Leave a Domain

To leave the Domain, sign in to your Local Account, click *Start > Settings > System > About* and then select Disconnect from the organization.

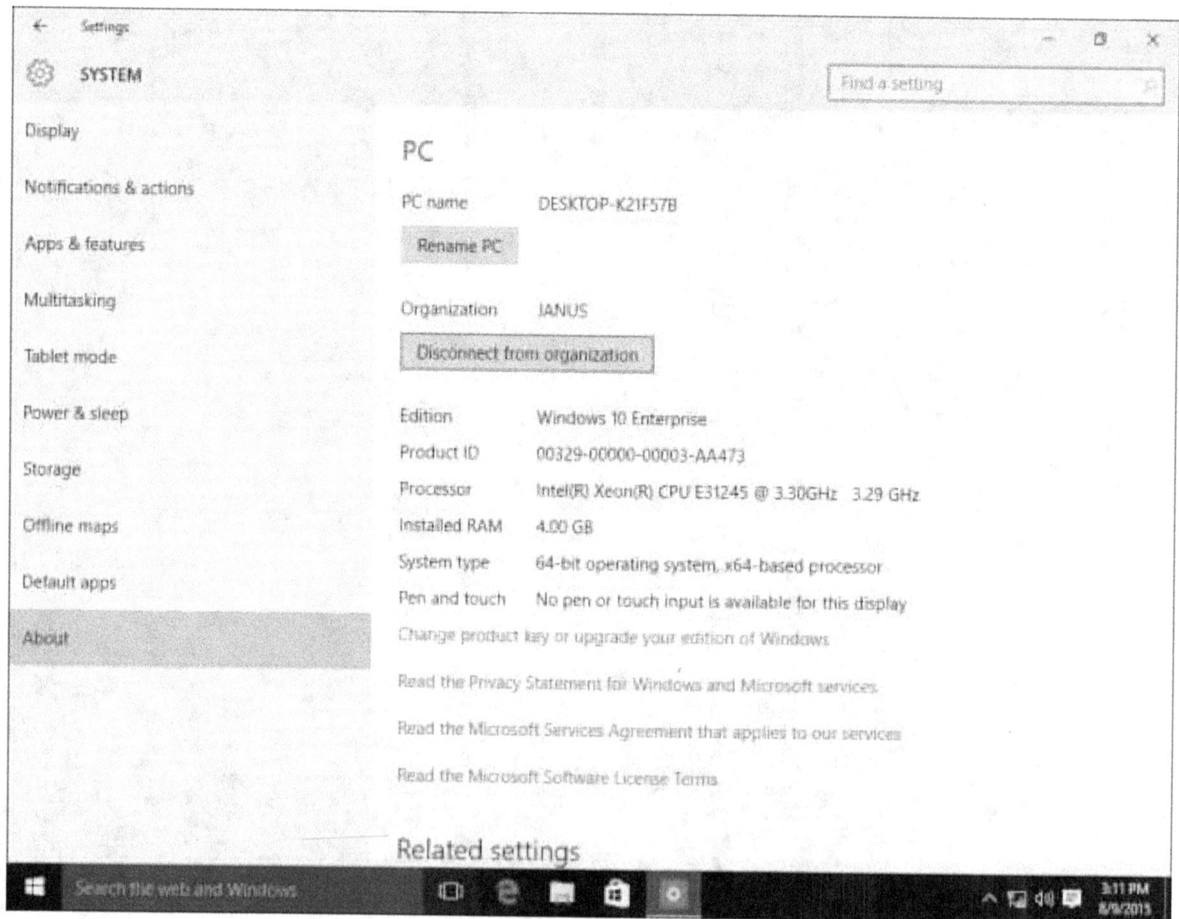

CHPTER 5: Types of Servers in Computing

The usage of servers may be defined as providing data to users. Servers can be used to manage a network, share files or programs, host databases, and host web pages and e-mail.

The server is similar to personal computers. Its components are the processor (CPU), memory (RAM), and hard disk. Servers contain hardware and programs that are tailored to their intended function. As a result, the target server type is determined by the intended purpose.

In this article, we will outline the most prevalent types of servers used today. The most widely used types of servers are as follows:

1. Web Server
2. Database Server
3. Email Server
4. Web Proxy Server
5. DNS Server
6. FTP Server
7. File Server
8. DHCP Server
9. Cloud Server
10. Application Server
11. Print Server
12. NTP Server
13. Radius Server
14. Syslog Server
15. Physical Server

1. Web Server

The server that is in charge of publishing a website on the internet is known as a **web server**. A server that provides hosting, also called **"hosting"**, over the internet protocol is called a **web server**. The renting of space required to publish Web pages on the Internet is referred to as "hosting". **Hosting** means putting pages, images, or documents meant for a website on a computer that internet users use to access them. Apache, Microsoft's Internet Information Server (IIS), and Nginx are the most popular web servers on the Internet.

Web Server
www. XT. Com

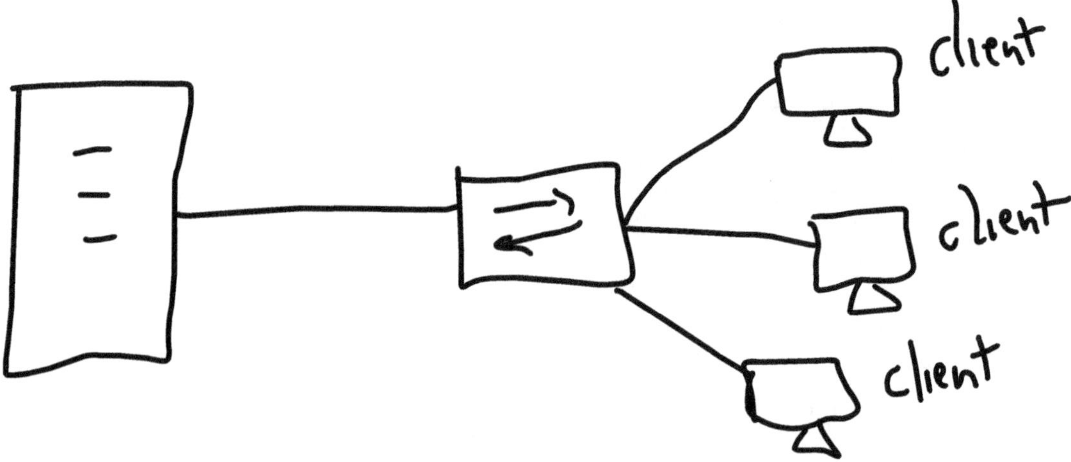

The data for each site you see on the internet is stored on another host, and software called Web Server. Web Server is used to efficiently use this computer. Web servers are typically made up of numerous software packages. Each of these software packages aids in the control of various functions. For example, the File Transfer Protocol (FTP) package that comes with web server software helps the server do FTP tasks. Similarly, numerous packages are available to perform a variety of tasks, such as serving emails, fulfilling download requests, and publishing web pages over HTTP.

The most common web servers are as follows:

- **Apache HTTP Server:** The Apache Software Foundation created the world's most popular web server. Apache is an open-source web server that can be installed on Linux, Unix, Windows, FreeBSD, Mac OS X, and many other operating systems. The Apache Web Server is used by over 60% of web server computers.

- **Internet Information Services:** Microsoft's Internet Information Server (IIS) is a high-performance Web server.

- **Lighttpd:** Lighttpd, pronounced lighty, is a free web server that comes with the FreeBSD operating system. This open-source web server is quick, safe, and uses far less CPU power. Lighttpd may also be run on Windows, Mac OS X, Linux, and Solaris.

- **Nginx:** Nginx Web Server is a critical component in the client-server computing environment, providing business-critical information to client systems. Like Lighttpd, it is an <u>open-source</u> web server that is known for being fast and needing few resources and time to set up. It is mostly used for caching, streaming media, load balancing, managing static files, auto-indexing, and other similar tasks. Nginx handles requests on a single thread, employing an asynchronous technique rather than generating new processes for each request made by the user.

- **Sun Java System Web Server:** Sun Microsystems' web server is designed for medium and large websites. The server is free, but it is not open source. It, on the other hand, runs on Windows, Linux, and Unix platforms. The Sun Java System web server supports a wide range of Web 2.0 languages, scripts, and technologies, including JSP, Java Servlets, PHP, Perl, Python, Ruby on Rails, ASP, and Coldfusion.

2. Database Server

A **database server** manages a database and provides database services to clients. The server manages data access and retrieval as well as the completion of client requests. A database server is a computer that runs database software and is dedicated to providing database services. A database server is made up of hardware and software that is used to run a database.

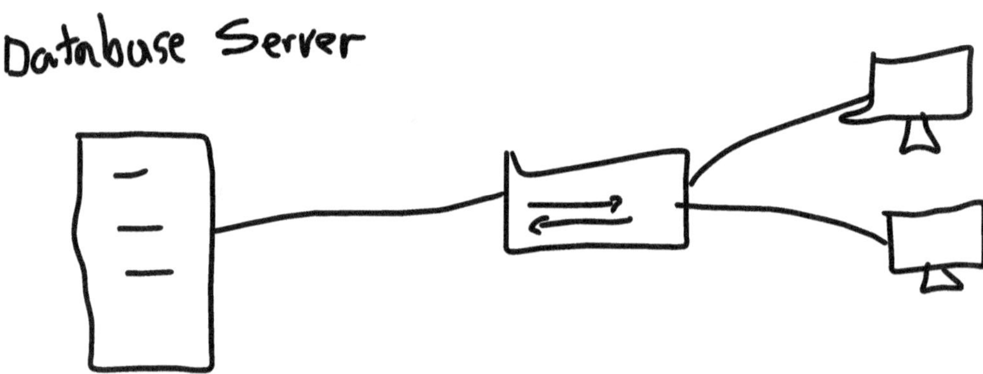

Database servers have a variety of applications. Among them are:

- Dealing with large amounts of data regularly. Database servers shine in client-server architectures where clients process data frequently.
- Managing the DBMS's (database management system) recovery and security. Database servers enforce the constraints specified in the DBMS. The server manages and controls all <u>clients</u> connected to it, as well as all database access and control requests.
- Concurrent access control is provided. Database servers provide a multi-user environment in which multiple users can access the database at the same time while maintaining security and concealing the DBMS from clients.
- Application and non-database file storage Database servers are a much more efficient solution for some organizations than file servers.

Most database servers use the client-server model. They get requests from client devices and their users and then send back the response that was asked for. Database servers are powerful machines that can connect to multiple databases and serve resources to clients, sometimes with the help of application servers and web servers that act as middlemen. Databases, for example, can provide resources to clients in the absence of a web or application server (usually on-premises).

Here are a few well-known examples of database servers.

- **Oracle:** Oracle is the most commonly used database for object-relational database administration, and the most recent version is 12c (12 Cloud Computing). It supports various <u>Linux</u>, Windows, and UNIX versions.

- **IBM DB2:** IBM DB2 was designed in C, C++, and Assembly and was initially released in 1983. Its setup and installation procedures are straightforward, as is data access. As a result, it aids in the storing of large volumes of data, up to petabytes.

- **Microsoft SQL Server:** This server was first introduced in 1989. It is written in several languages, including Assembly, C, Linux, and C++. It can run Linux and Windows. It enables multiple users to use the same database at the same time.

- **MySQL:** MySQL is becoming more popular for many web-based applications. It is available as both a freeware and a premium edition.

- **SAP HANA:** It was created by SAP SE and can manage both SAP and non-SAP data. It is capable of supporting OLTP, OLAP, and SQL. It can communicate with a wide range of different apps.

- **MS Access:** It is only compatible with Microsoft Windows. Because this database management system is inexpensive, it is commonly used for e-commerce websites.

3. Email Server

A mail server, also known as an email server, is a computer system that sends and receives emails. When you send an email, it passes through several servers before arriving at its destination. While this process is quick and efficient, there is a significant amount of complexity involved in sending and receiving emails.

For a computer to work as a mail server, mail server software must be installed on it. The system administrator then uses this software to create and manage email accounts for any of the domains hosted on the server. Aside from that, you have protocols. Protocols are network software rules that enable computers to connect to networks from anywhere, allowing you to shop online, send emails, and so on.

Mail servers are classified into two types: outgoing mail servers and incoming mail servers. SMTP, or Simple Messages Transfer Protocol, servers handle outgoing mail. Incoming mail servers are classified into two groups. Messages are kept on the server while using IMAP. When using POP3, messages are often stored on a device, such as your computer or mobile phone. IMAP, in general, is more complicated and adaptable than POP3.

- **SMTP:** The SMTP protocol handles all incoming mail and sends emails. SMTP stands for Simple Mail Transfer Protocol and refers to the outgoing mail server. Consider SMTP to be the transport of your email across networks. Your emails would be useless without them.

- *IMAP / POP.* There are two types of incoming mail servers–POP3 and IMAP. Post Office Protocol version 3 (POP3) servers are well-known for getting your computer's Inbox contents. IMAP servers, which stand for Internet Message Access Protocol, are used for one-way mailbox synchronization. IMAP is used as an additional protocol retrieval application on a mail server. And, while there are newer POP versions with more functionality, the recommended protocol remains POP3 since it is straightforward, has a high success rate, and gets the job done with the fewest problems. You can even download your emails and read them offline. Your email would not reach your machine if one of these protocols was not functioning properly.

A mail server, in its most basic form, collects email and forwards it to its intended recipients. It can be thought of as a computer serving as an e-mail office, allowing control of e-mail transmission over a network using various protocols. How an e-mail server works are explained below:

1. **Making a connection to the SMTP server:** When you send an email, your email service or provider will connect to the SMTP server, such as Gmail, Exchange, Office 365, Expert Mail, or Zimbra. This SMTP server is associated with your domain and has a unique address. At this point, your email provider will send crucial information to the SMTP server, such as your email address, message body, and recipient's email address.

2. **Taking care of the recipient's email domain:** The SMTP server identifies and processes the recipient's email address in this phase. If you email someone else within your firm, the message will be sent directly to the IMAP or POP3 server. If you are sending the message to another company, the SMTP server must speak with the email server of that company.

3. **Determining the IP address of the recipient:** At this point, your SMTP server needs to connect to the recipient's server using DNS (Domain Name System). DNS functions similarly to a translation mechanism. It aids in the conversion of the recipient's domain name into an IP address. To function effectively, SMTP requires an IP address to forward the message to the recipient's server.

4. **Email delivery:** Everything is not as straightforward as it appears. In general, your email will be routed through several SMTP servers before arriving at the recipient's SMTP server. When the recipient receives the email, SMTP validates it before forwarding it to the IMAP or POP3 server. The email is then processed in a queue until it is available for the recipient to access.

4. Web Proxy Server

People rarely consider how complicated the internet is. The threat of crimes such as identity theft and data security breaches is growing. To protect themselves, many people employ proxy servers or Virtual Private Networks (VPN). A **proxy server** is a web server that serves as a conduit between a client program, such as a browser, and the actual server. It sends queries to the accurate server on the client's behalf and sometimes fulfills the claim itself. Web proxy servers offer two key functions: they filter requests and increase performance. In addition, there are reverse proxy servers that reside between web servers and web clients. Requests from web clients are routed through reverse proxy servers to web servers. They are used to cache pictures and pages to drastically minimize the strain on web servers.

There are various reasons why an individual or company may use web proxy servers. Limit internet access. You can control and keep an eye on your kids' internet use as an individual by using proxy servers. It operates by blocking undesirable websites and preventing access to pornographic content. Proxy servers are also used by businesses to block and regulate internet access. They use this to keep employees from surfing the web while at work. Alternatively, they track all web requests, which shows which websites employees visit and how much time they spend online.

Benefits of using a web proxy server are as follows:

- **More privacy:** By altering your IP address and other identifying data on your computer, proxy servers allow you to access the internet more discreetly. Proxy servers protect your personal information, so the server does not know who made the request, keeping your surfing activity and browser history secret.
- **Access to restricted websites:** Material providers restricts their content for a variety of reasons, including location, which is effectively the IP addresses. A web proxy server, on the other hand, allows you to log on to a restricted service by making it appear that you are at a different location.
- **Improved performance and bandwidth savings:** Using effective web proxy servers, businesses may save bandwidth and increase loading rates. To preserve the most recent copy of a website, proxy servers cache pictures and web data. Caches enable a proxy server to obtain the most recent copy of popular sites, saving traffic and improving network efficiency.
- **Enhanced Security:** Efficient proxy servers encrypt your online requests to keep them safe from prying eyes and to safeguard your transactions. Proxy servers are used to avoid attacks from known malware sites. VPNs are also used by businesses to boost security and

allow remote users to access the company network. Web proxy servers are important in cybersecurity for both individuals and organizations.

Let's have a look at some of the most popular and greatest online proxy servers:

- **SmartProxy:** Best for quickly configuring proxies in Firefox and Chrome. Smartproxy provides a home proxy network that allows you to send an infinite number of connection requests at the same time. This enables your scraper to quickly visit a large number of web pages. You can create a different proxy user for each job. Each of these proxy users will have their login information. This service makes it extremely simple to set up proxies. Smartproxy provides extensive documentation that covers everything you'll need to know about setting up and installing proxies.
- **Bright Data:** Ideal for creating data-driven business decisions since it aids in the unlocking of any website and the collection of reliable data. Bright Data includes a Proxy Manager that allows you to manage all of your proxies from a single interface. The Proxy Manager is a free and open-source application. It includes scraping capabilities. Bright Data provides Data Center Proxies, ISP Proxies, Residential Proxies, Mobile Proxies, Web Unlocker, and other solutions.
- **HMA:** Best for browsing anonymously. For anonymous browsing, HMA offers a free proxy server. It enables access to banned websites from anywhere in the world and includes features like private browsing in a single tab, IP masking in a single tab, and safe online banking on any network, among others. We may use it on any device, making online games and apps safer.
- **Whoer:** The best tool for fast-changing IP addresses and unblocking websites for free. Whoer provides web proxy, Internet speed testing, online ping test checker, domain & IP verification, and DNS leak testing services. Its web proxy provides a quick and free solution to

change your IP address, unblock websites, and acquire web anonymity. Services are available in various countries.

- Hide.me: The best VPN for speed and privacy protection. Hide.me is a web proxy service that offers apps for all platforms as well as secure VPN protocols. It adheres to a stringent no-logs policy. The premium edition includes dynamic port forwarding, a fixed IP address, and streaming capability. It offers a free browser extension for Firefox and Chrome.

5. DNS Server

The Domain Name System (DNS) is the Internet's telephone directory. DNS is responsible for finding the correct IP address for websites when users enter their domain names, such as 'google.com' or 'nytimes.com,' into web browsers.

The addresses are then used by browsers to communicate with origin servers or CDN edge servers to access website information. All this is possible by __DNS__ servers, which are specialized machines for answering DNS queries.

To resolve names, the DNS system has resolving systems. Name resolvers are used to find IP addresses associated with domain names. DNS clients are the people who use resolvers. A DNS system can have many name resolvers. As a result, if one of them becomes incapacitated, the others take over and ensure that communication is not disrupted.

When you type a domain name into your browser and log in, your browser first asks your operating system for the domain name, which does not answer. Then it asks your modem and continues to ask until it reaches the Internet service provider and the main DNS servers.

If the matching DNS server database contains an equivalent of this domain name, it will respond to the IP address, and your browser will get this response in a fraction of a second and speak with the server where the relevant domain name is hosted. The data transfer then begins, and the required webpage is displayed in your browser.

In an uncached DNS query, four servers collaborate to supply an IP address to the client: recursive resolvers, root nameservers, TLD nameservers, and authoritative nameservers. The DNS recursor (also called the DNS resolver) is a server that accepts the DNS client's query and then contacts other DNS servers to locate the proper IP address. When the resolver receives the client's request, it acts like a client, contacting the other three types of DNS servers in search of the correct IP address. The resolver begins by querying the root nameserver. The root server is the first step in converting human-readable names to IP addresses (resolving). The root server then responds to the resolver by supplying the address of a top-level domain (TLD) DNS server (such as.com or.net) that includes data for its domains.

6. FTP Server

FTP is a network protocol that is used to transfer files between a client and a server on a computer network. FTP is a well-known protocol that was developed in the 1970s to allow two computers to transfer data over the internet. One computer serves as the server, storing information, while the other serves as the client, sending or requesting files from the server. The FTP protocol's primary mode of communication is normally port 21. On <u>port</u> 21, an FTP server will accept client connections. FTP servers, as well as the more secure SFTP Server software, carry out two basic functions: "Put" and "Get."

An FTP Server is useful if you have remote employees who need to submit non-confidential material (such as timesheets), or if you wish to allow your clients to obtain white papers and documentation. If you're transferring non-sensitive data with a business partner who requires FTP or SFTP, you can rapidly set up a server to accept their data transfer. Some people even utilize FTP servers for offsite backup so they can access their data if something happens to their files physically.

Furthermore, backup apps frequently write to an FTP or SFTP Server; for example, if you are backing up your Cisco Unified Call Manager (CUCM), the data must be backed up to an SFTP Server, such as Titan FTP Server.

FTP Server is defined as an infrastructure that enables organizations with various file transmission options. FTP servers, which have numerous advantages in this regard, are particularly appealing to organizations looking to enhance their multimedia experience. In addition to options such as quick file transmission and integrated usage options, the following are the highlights of FTP server advantages:

- **Options for Effective File Sharing**: Businesses that put up FTP infrastructure speed up file transfer between business machines via their clients. Devices have multimedia capabilities that allow them to communicate efficiently with one another. As a result, needless data transfer stages are disabled.

- **Providing Data Security**: Because FTP performs all data transfer activities through the in-house client, it also protects against outside <u>cybersecurity</u> breaches. The fact that the client in the company communicates with the company devices across the common network also aids in isolating the network from external variables.

- **Interaction across a Common Network**: Another significant benefit of an FTP server for organizations is that it enables devices to connect in an integrated manner across a single network. As a result, the company's gadgets can communicate indefinitely with the client. As a result, communication between company devices continues at its peak.

7. File Server

A file server is a central server in a computer network that serves file systems or portions of file systems to clients connected to the network. As a result, file servers provide users with a central storage location for files on internal data media that is available to all authorized clients. The server administrator establishes rigorous guidelines for which users have which access rights: For example, the configuration or file authorizations of the individual file system allow the admin to specify which files a certain user or user group may access and open, as well as whether data can only be seen or additionally added, altered, or deleted.

Users can access files over the local network as well as remotely when file servers are linked to the internet and set up properly. This allows users to view and store files on the file server when they are on the move. All current operating systems, such as Windows, Linux, or macOS, can be used on a file server, but the network devices must be compatible with the operating system. However, file servers are used for more than just file storage and administration. They are also frequently used as a backup server and as a repository for applications that must be available to numerous network members.

Clients can only access a distant file system through file servers. They can hold any form of material, such as executables, documents, images, or movies. They typically store data as binary blobs or files. This implies they don't do any further indexing or processing on the files they store. However, there may be other plugins or server operations that can give additional functionalities. A file server does not have built-in methods for interacting with data and relies on the client to do so. Because databases only deal with structured data that is retrieved via a query, they are not considered file servers.

File servers usually incorporate extra capabilities that allow several users to use them at the same time: Permission management is used to control who has access to certain files and who has the authority to alter or delete them. Locking a file prevents several people from editing the same file at the same time. Resolution of conflicts; preservation of data integrity in the case of file overwriting. By duplicating data to numerous servers in different places, a distributed file system may make data redundant and highly accessible.

For many businesses, employing a file server is worthwhile for a variety of reasons. The first advantage is, obviously, centrality, which assures that any authorized network participant has access to the stored data.

This enables collaborative work on certain files. Conflicts between multiple versions of a document may be virtually eliminated since certain operations, such as editing or deleting, are disabled for other users as soon as you access a file. If users have to share the needed files on their system or send them via removable media, it will be significantly more time-consuming and inconvenient – and it will almost certainly result in different file versions.

Another significant benefit of employing file servers is that it alleviates the burden on client resources. Except for personal papers, almost all corporate data and backups can be saved on the file server, depending on how the organization intends to use the file repository. And, with the proper arrangement (directories, folders, etc.), users get a far better perspective of the full file inventory.

If the file server is set up for remote access through the internet, the files are also available on the go, similar to an online storage service. Unlike cloud service, however, the organization maintains complete control over the files and their security at all times. This is a significant benefit over third-party solutions.

8. DHCP Server

A DHCP Server is a network server that gives and assigns IP addresses, default gateways, and other network information to client devices on an automatic basis. To reply to client broadcast inquiries, it uses the standard protocol known as Dynamic Host Configuration Protocol or DHCP.

A DHCP server automatically sends the network parameters required for clients to communicate successfully on the network. Without it, the network administrator must manually configure each client that connects to the network, which can be time-consuming, especially in big networks.

DHCP servers typically assign a unique dynamic IP address to each client, which changes when the client's lease for that IP address expires.

Each device connected to the Internet on an IP network must be allocated a unique IP address. DHCP allows network managers to centrally monitor and assign IP addresses. When a computer is relocated, it can automatically give a new IP address to it. DHCP automates the process of allocating IP addresses, reducing both the time necessary for device configuration and deployment and the likelihood of configuration errors. A DHCP server can also manage the setups of several network segments. When a network segment's configuration changes, an administrator merely needs to update the relevant settings on the DHCP server.

Configuration of a dependable IP address. DHCP reduces manual IP address configuration problems, such as typographical errors, and address conflicts caused by assigning an IP address to more than one computer at the same time. Network administration has been simplified. To reduce network administration, DHCP supports the following features:

- TCP/IP configuration is centralized and automated. The ability to define TCP/IP setups from a single point of contact.
- The ability to use DHCP to assign a wide variety of additional TCP/IP configuration parameters. The efficient management of IP address changes for clients that need to be updated often, such as portable devices that roam across a wireless network.

9. Cloud Server

A cloud server is a pooled, centralized server resource that is hosted and distributed across a network -typically the Internet- and may be accessed by multiple users on demand. Cloud servers provide all of the same services as traditional physical servers, including processing power, storage, and applications. Cloud servers can be situated anywhere in the world and provide remote services via a <u>cloud</u> computing environment. Traditional dedicated server hardware, on the other hand, is often installed on premises for the sole use of one firm.

Because any software issue is isolated from your environment, a cloud server is used. Other cloud servers will have no impact on yours, and vice versa. In contrast to physical servers, another user overloading their cloud server does not influence your cloud server. Cloud servers are dependable, fast, and secure. Because they do not have the hardware issues that physical servers do, they are likely to be the most stable alternative for firms that want to keep their IT expenditure as low as possible. Cloud servers provide greater service at a lower cost. You'll get more resources and faster service than you would with an equivalent physical server. It is relatively simple and quick to upgrade by adding memory and storage space, and it is also less expensive.

10. Application Server

An application server is software that runs on the server and is written by a server programmer to provide business logic for any application. This server might be part of a network or a dispersed network. Server programs are typically used to give services to client programs that are either on the same system or a network. Application servers reduce traffic while increasing security. It is not possible to achieve ideal web server agility by handling both HTTP requests from web clients and passing or storing resources from numerous websites. Application servers fill this need with a powerful architecture designed to handle dynamic online content requests.

Application servers provide programs with protection and redundancy. The task of conserving and replicating application architecture across the network becomes more achievable once deployed between a database and a web server. The extra step between potentially harmful web connections and the database server's crown jewels offers an extra degree of security. Because application servers can handle business logic queries, an attempted SQL injection is more difficult. Some of the advantages of Application Servers can be listed as follows:

- Provides a framework for managing all components and operating services such as session management and synchronous and asynchronous client notifications. It becomes incredibly simple to install programs in one location.
- Any configuration change, such as changing the Database server, may be made centrally from a single place. They make it simple to deliver patches and security upgrades.
- It allows you to route requests to other servers based on their availability. Load balancing is used to accomplish this.
- It ensures the security of applications. It allows for fault tolerance as well as recovery/failover recovery.
- It saves us a lot of time if we have to install a duplicate of settings on each machine manually. It has transaction support.
- Because it is built on the <u>client-server</u> concept, the application server dramatically enhances application performance.

11. Print Server

A print server is a software program, network device, or computer that manages print requests and provides end users and network administrators with printer queue status information. Print servers are used in big business networks as well as small or home office (SOHO) networks.

A single dedicated computer operating as a print server in a large firm manages hundreds of printers. A print server in a small office is generally a customized plug-in board or tiny network device the size of a hub that serves the same function as a dedicated print server while freeing up critical disk space on the workplace's limited number of PCs.

A print server, like other servers, works on the client-server architecture, receiving and processing user requests. Physical print servers, as shown in the diagram above, sit on the back end of an organization's network and connect directly to network printers, retaining control over the print queue. The print server handles devices to request information, such as file and print requirements. While most printing occurs within workplace networks, print servers are available to external network clients (typically via approved login).

Print-server software can be deployed on a network file server or your computer. UNIX-based operating systems such as Mac OS X and Linux, by default, employ the CUPS, or Common UNIX Printing System, which includes built-in print-server functionality. A print server can also be a single-purpose network hardware device that connects to a printer directly. Some printers include print-server technology that allows them to connect directly to a network router or switch.

There are several ways to connect a printer to a print server. It might be physically linked to a file server or client computer by a parallel, serial, or USB connection. Dedicated network print-server hardware devices connect to a printer directly through a parallel or USB connection and the network wirelessly or by an RJ45, Ethernet cable connection. Printers with built-in print-server hardware can connect to the network through wireless or Ethernet.

Before your document is finally printed and ready for pickup, the print server, and your computer's operating system must locate the printer you want to use, establish a network communication path to it, package your document into a data format that the printer can directly understand, send the formatted data to the printer, and monitor the printer's progress as it prints your document. Finally, it informs you whether or not the printing procedure was successful. The printer drivers installed on your computer, as well as network printing protocols such as IPP (Internet Printing Protocol) and LPR (Line Printer Remote protocol), manage the complex, low-level details for you.

While printers are slower output devices than hard drives or CD writers, print-server software may compensate by keeping your document in a temporary file called a spool and only sending out bits of your document at the pace at which your printer can reliably handle them. If you send numerous documents to the printer or if many users try to print at the same time, print servers installed on network file servers can queue each page. The printer server transmits documents in the queue to the printer in a systematic, dependable, first-come, first-served manner.

12. NTP Server

Network Time Protocol (NTP) is an internet protocol that is used to synchronize with computer clock time sources in a network. It belongs to and is one of the earliest components of the TCP/IP suite. The word NTP refers to both the protocol and the client-server applications that operate on computers. NTP was invented in 1981 by David Mills, a professor at the University of Delaware. It is intended to be extremely fault-tolerant and scalable, while also allowing temporal synchronization.

The NTP time synchronization procedure consists of three steps:

1. The NTP client conducts a time-request exchange with the NTP server.

2. The client may then determine the connection latency and its local offset, as well as change its local time to match the clock on the server's computer.

3. Typically, six exchanges over a five to ten-minute period are required to set the clock.

Once synced, the client refreshes the clock approximately every 10 minutes, needing only a single message exchange in addition to client-server synchronization. This transaction takes place on port 123 of the User Datagram Protocol (UDP). NTP also provides peer computer clock broadcast synchronization.

Accurate time for all devices on a computer network is critical for several reasons; even a fraction of a second difference can cause problems. The following are some instances of how NTP is used:

- Coordinated times are required for distributed procedures to guarantee proper sequences are followed.

- Consistent timekeeping across the network is required for security procedures.
- File system changes performed across several machines rely on synchronized clock times.
- To monitor performance and fix issues, network acceleration and network management systems rely on the precision of timestamps.

13. Radius Server

RADIUS (Remote Authentication Dial-In User Service) is a networking protocol that connects clients and servers. RADIUS is a computer network authentication, authorization, and accounting (AAA) management protocol. RADIUS is a UDP-based protocol that authenticates users using a shared secret.

The RADIUS protocol employs a RADIUS Server and RADIUS Clients.

- RADIUS server: checks users' credentials against a database of usernames and passwords. It also grants network resources access.
- RADIUS client: a network-connected device that provides its credentials to the RADIUS server. After that, the RADIUS server authenticates the client and returns authorization or access control information to it. To establish an authenticated session, the RADIUS server, and client exchange messages. This session is used for duties such as authorization, bookkeeping, and others.

To authenticate remote users, a RADIUS server consults a central database. When access is allowed, RADIUS acts as a client-server protocol, authenticating each user with a unique encryption key. The particular nature of the RADIUS ecosystem determines how a RADIUS server operates. An overview of RADIUS servers is provided below.

1. First, the user authenticates with the network access server (NAS).

2. The network access server will then request a username and password or a challenge (CHAP).

3. The user responds.

4. When the RADIUS client receives the user's response, it sends the username and the uniquely encrypted password to the RADIUS server.

5. The user is accepted or rejected by the RADIUS server.

RADIUS servers are well known for their AAA (Authentication, Authorization, and Accounting) capabilities. The key benefits of a RADIUS server's centralized AAA capabilities are increased security and efficiency. RADIUS servers enable each firm to protect the privacy and security of both the system and each user.

The RADIUS server offers a variety of authentication techniques. When supplied with the user's username and original password, it can support PAP, CHAP, MS-CHAP, EAP, EAP TLS, UNIX login, and other authentication protocols.

- **PAP**: Password Authentication Protocol (PAP) authentication configures authentication using PPP configuration files and the PAP database. PAP works similarly to the UNIX login software, however, PAP does not allow the user shell access.
- **CHAP**: Challenge-Handshake Authentication Protocol (CHAP) authentication employs challenge and response, which means that the authenticator challenges the caller (authenticates) to prove their identity. The challenge includes the authenticator's unique ID and a random number. The caller generates the answer (handshake) to send

to the peer using the ID, random number, and CHAP security credentials.

- **MS-CHAP**: MS-CHAP is the Microsoft Challenge-Handshake Authentication Protocol (CHAP). It is used as an authentication option in Microsoft's PPTP protocol implementation for VPNs.
- **EAP**: Extensible Authentication Protocol (EAP) is a wireless network and point-to-point connection authentication mechanism.

14. Syslog Server

The System Logging Protocol (Syslog) is a standard message format used by network devices to connect with a logging server. It was created primarily to make monitoring network devices simple. Devices can use a Syslog agent to send out notification messages under a variety of scenarios.

These log messages comprise a timestamp, a severity rating, a device ID (including IP address), and event-specific information. Though it has flaws, the Syslog protocol is extensively used because it is simple to construct and very open-ended, allowing for a variety of proprietary implementations and hence the ability to monitor practically any connected device.

The Syslog standard specifies three layers:

- **Syslog Content Layer:** This is the content in the event message. It includes several data items such as facility codes and severity ratings.

- **Syslog Application Layer:** The message is generated, interpreted, routed, and stored in this layer.

- **Syslog Transport Layer:** This layer is responsible for sending messages across a network.

When debugging difficulties, log information is quite useful. For example, if some users report a network outage, such as the recent Facebook, WhatsApp, and Instagram outages, we can simply scan through all of the log data to check if there were any difficulties. Data retention is another advantage of centrally keeping log information. It can give temporary information required to restore the system's previous status after a failure.

Syslog messages are transmitted through User Datagram Protocol (UDP) port 514. Because UDP is a connectionless protocol, messages are neither acknowledged nor guaranteed to arrive. This can be a disadvantage, but it also makes the system basic and easy to manage.

Syslog messages are frequently in human-readable format, but they do not have to be. Each message has a priority level in its header, which is a mix of code for the process of the device creating the message and a severity level. The process codes, known as "facilities," are based on UNIX. Severity levels vary from 0 (emergency) to 1 (urgent attention required), with informational and debug messages falling somewhere in between. These two codes, when combined, enable rapid classification of Syslog messages.

15. Physical Server

Some servers are solely utilized for specific functions. An application server, for example, just hosts the webpage. Physical servers are easy to use for a wide range of network tasks because of their software and hardware. Some of those transactions are:

- Operating system updates
- Services for firewalls
- Anti-spam software
- Antivirus software
- Defense against DDoS assaults
- DNS hosting
- Intrusion detection
- SNMP management
- Database administration
- Backups and restoration
- Security Procedures

CHAPTER 6 remove Roles and Features in Windows Server

IT admins can use the Server Manager on a GUI-based Windows Server to easily remove roles and features. In this post, we will walk you through the process of **how to remove Roles and Features** in Windows Server.

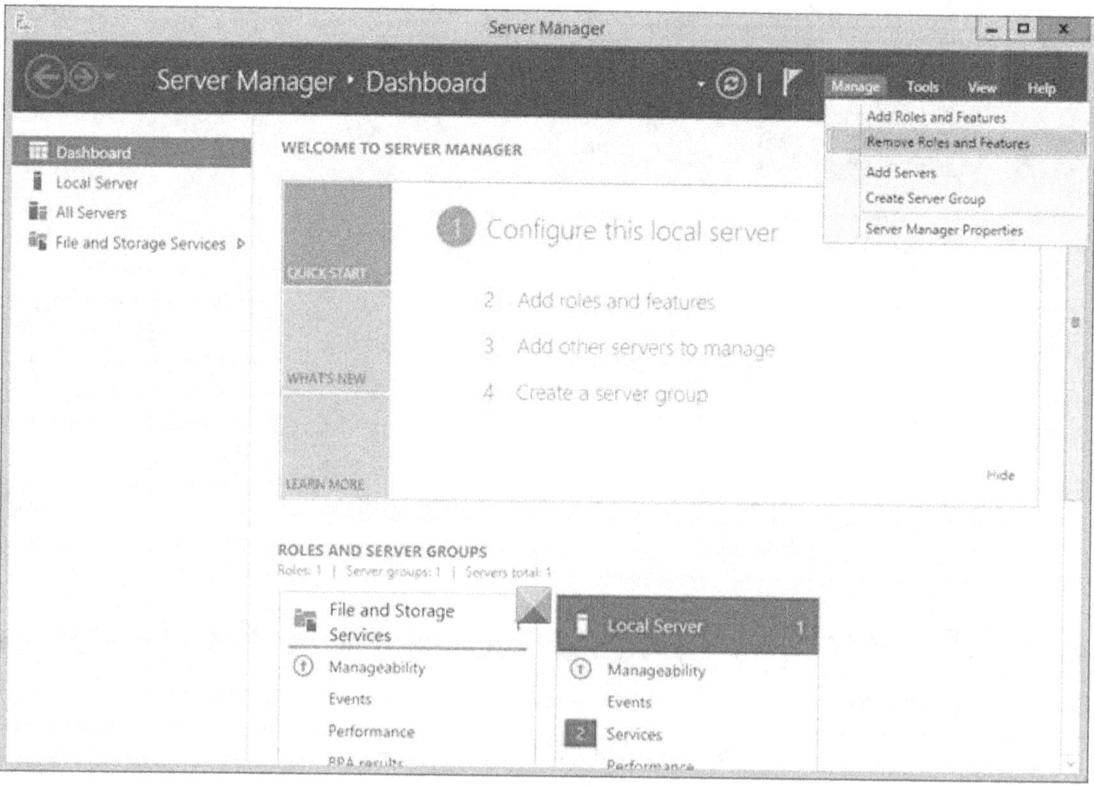

Before we jump into the subject matter proper, below is the prerequisite check;

- Plan on what you might want to do with role data — you can either save or delete it.
- You may want to plan and migrate role data to another server.
- Domain users must be informed about the potential interruption of services, as users might be affected during the process and the server may need to be rebooted.

- You will have to schedule downtime for services that may be affected.

Once you have ticked all the boxes, you can now proceed to remove roles and features in the Windows server.

Remove Roles and Features in Windows Server

To remove Roles and Features in Windows Server, do the following:

- Open Server Manager.
- Click **Manage** > **Remove Roles and Features** to launch the Remove Roles and Features Wizard.
- Review the proposed instructions.
- When done, click on the **Next** button under *Before You Begin* section.
- Next, in the *Select destination server* page, select the server from which you want to remove roles and features.
- Next, in the *Remove server roles* page, uncheck the option for the role you want to remove.
- Click **Next**.
- Next, in the *Remove features* page, uncheck the feature you want to remove.
- Click **Next**.

- In the *Confirm removal selections* page, select the **Restart the destination server automatically if required** option.

The server will be automatically restarted without additional notifications when this option is selected, as most of the features or roles may require rebooting the server.

- Click **Yes** on the prompt that appears.
- Now, click the **Remove** button.

Windows Server will now remove the feature/role you selected — and the server might restart when the removal process is completed.

Manage Website on IIS Web Server — Windows Server 2022

Internet Information Services (IIS) is a web server created by Microsoft, this step by step tutorial covers how to Manage a Website on IIS Web Server. IIS web server accepts requests from remote client computers and returns the appropriate response. Web Server (IIS) provides a reliable, manageable, and scalable Web application infrastructure.

Prerequisite Required

- Install Internet Information Services(IIS)
- Computer Name: server1.test.com
- Operating System: Windows Server 2022 Datacenter

- IP Address: 192.168.0.2

Create a Website on IIS Webserver

1. Open the Server Manager dashboard, click Tools, and select Internet Information Services (IIS) Manager.

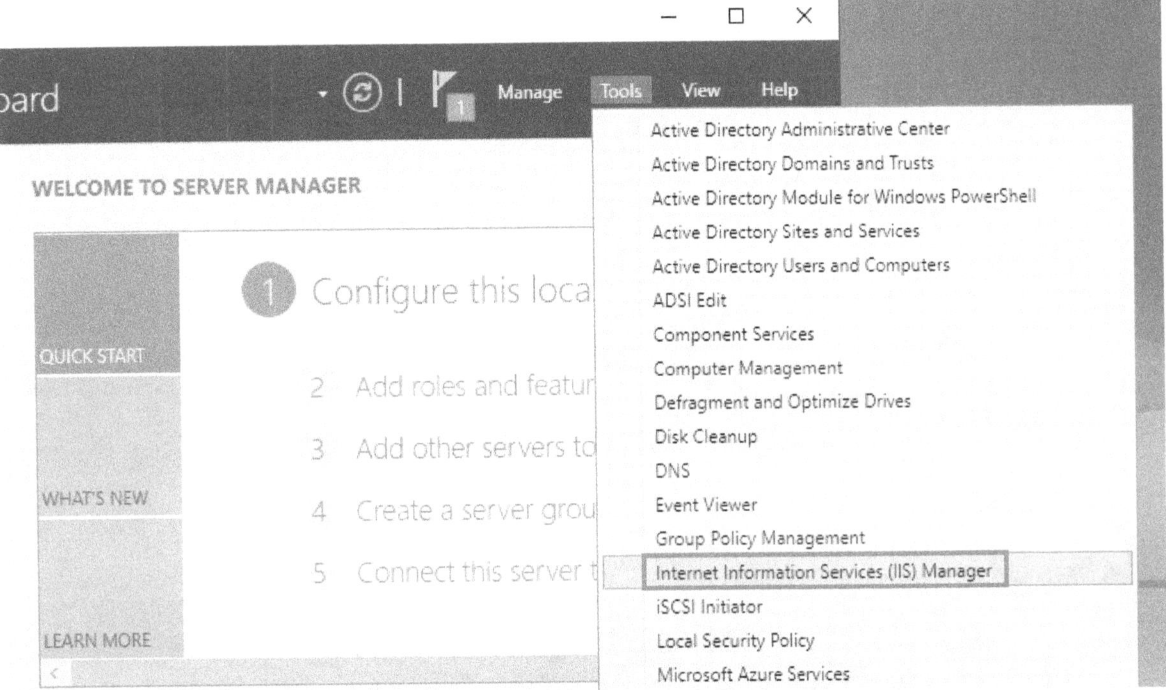

2. Right click on the Sites and select Add Website.

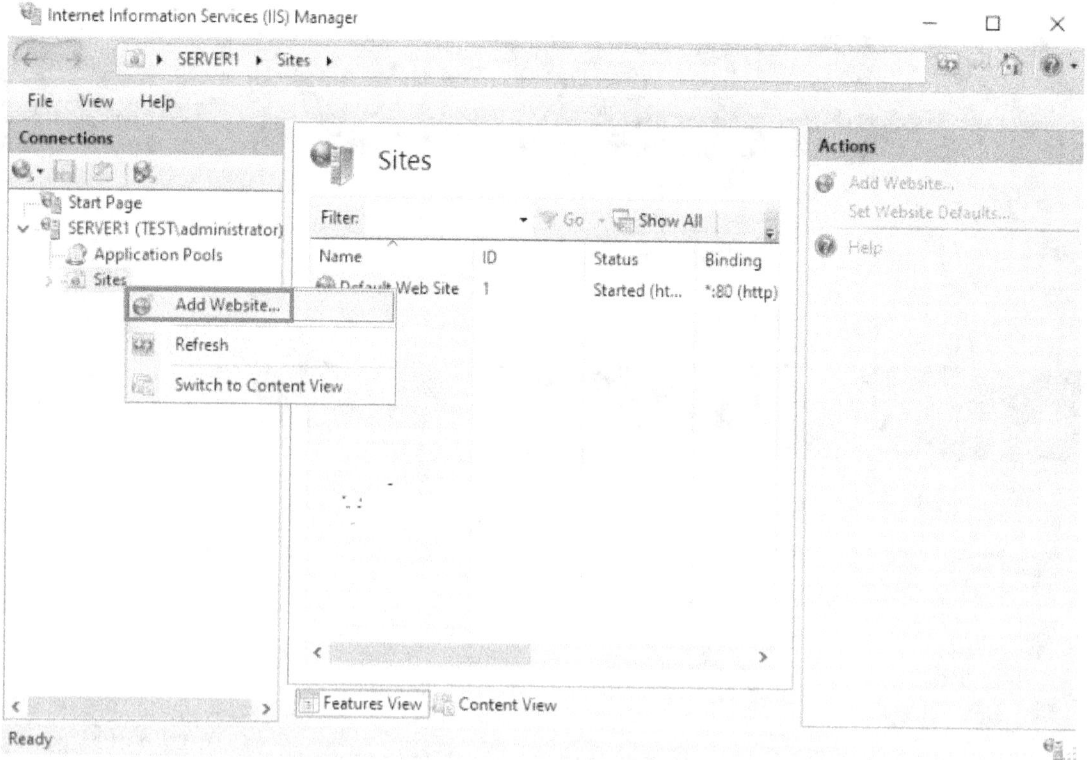

3. Configure the Site name, Content Directory, and Binding, and Click OK.

• Site name: testwebsite
• Physical path: c:\website
• Host name: server1.test.com

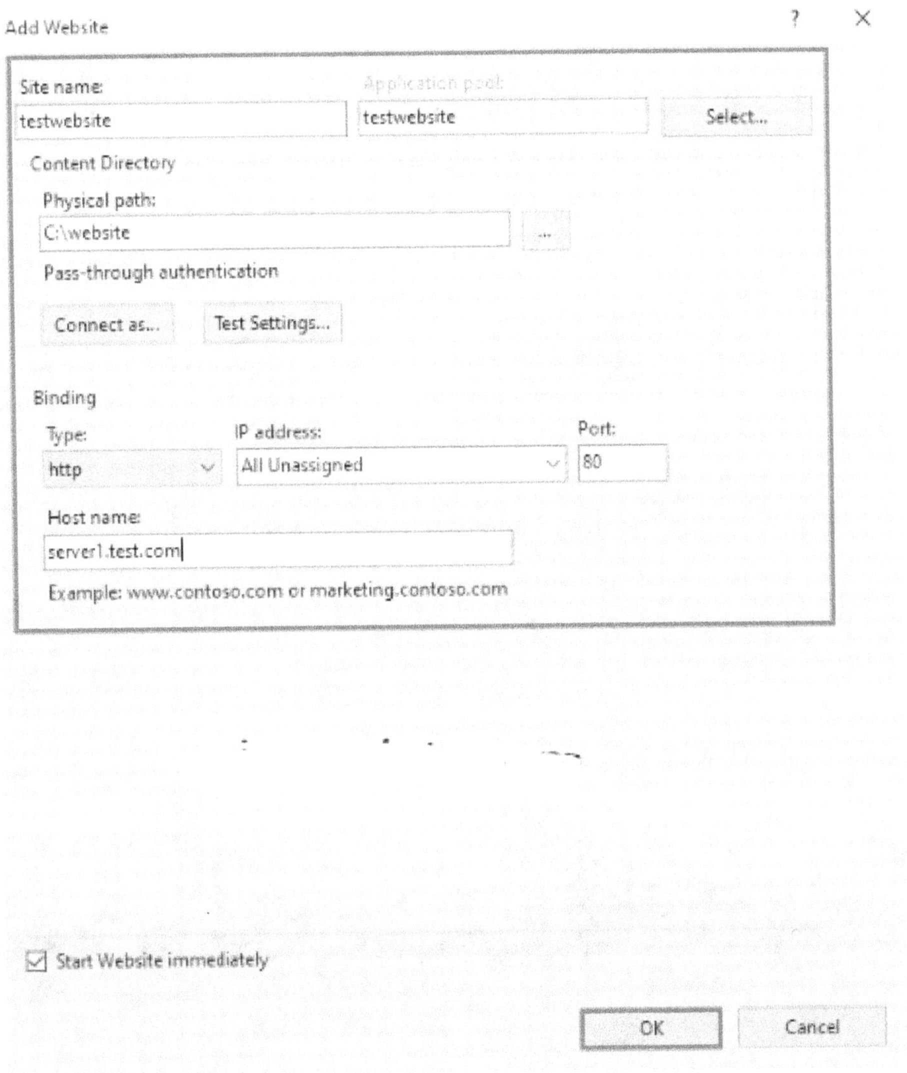

Add Website

Site name:
testwebsite

Application pool:
testwebsite

Select...

Content Directory

Physical path:
C:\website

Pass-through authentication

Connect as...   Test Settings...

Binding

Type:
http

IP address:
All Unassigned

Port:
80

Host name:
server1.test.com

Example: www.contoso.com or marketing.contoso.com

☑ Start Website immediately

OK   Cancel

4. Verify the website.

TEST WEBSITE

Stop Website on IIS Webserver

5. Right click on the Website, choose Manage Website, and Click Stop.

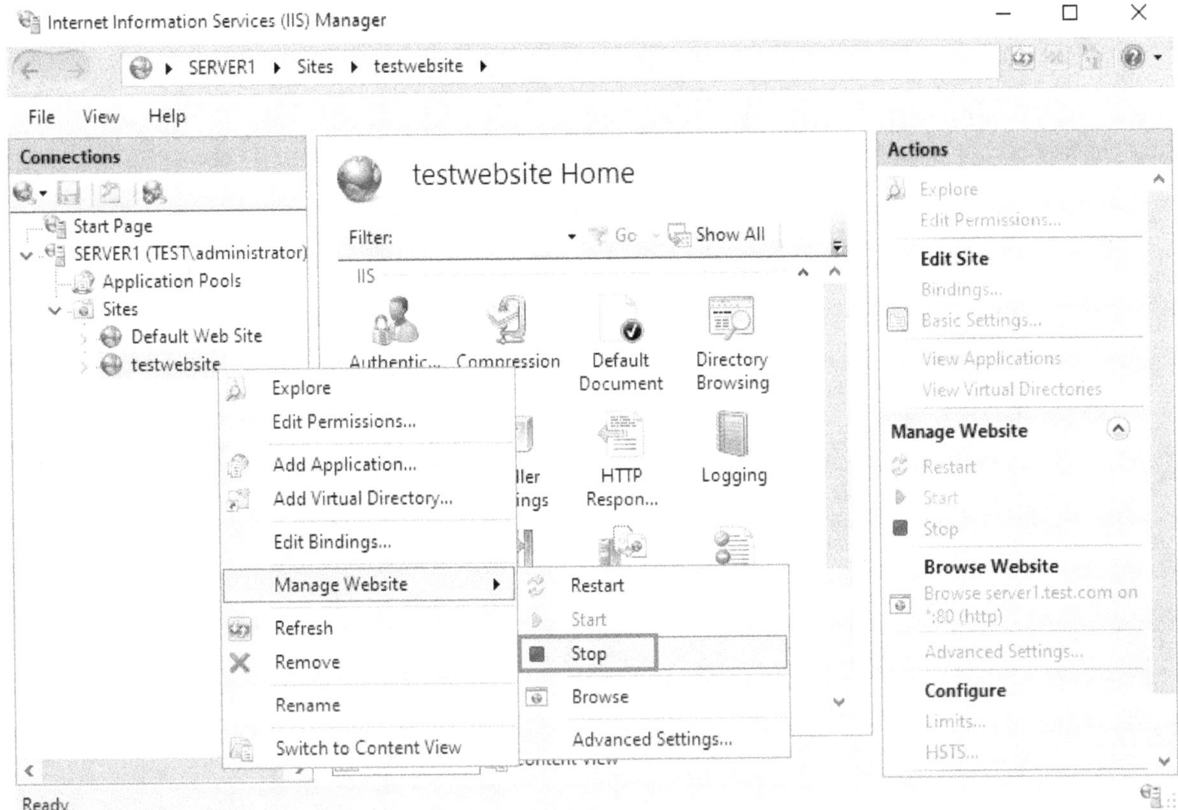

CHAPTER 7 : Start Website on IIS Webserver

6. Right click on the Website, choose Manage Website and Click Start.

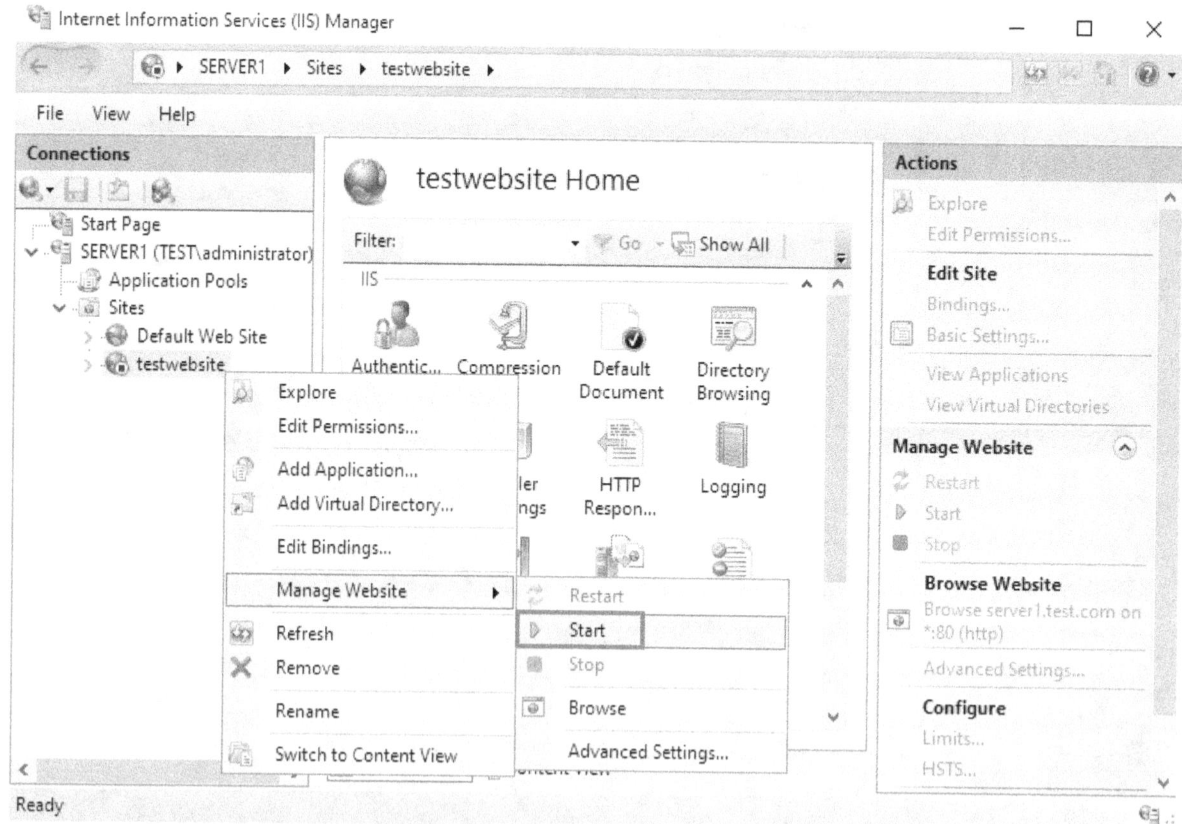

Restart the Website on IIS Webserver

7. Right click on the Website, choose Manage Website and Click Start.

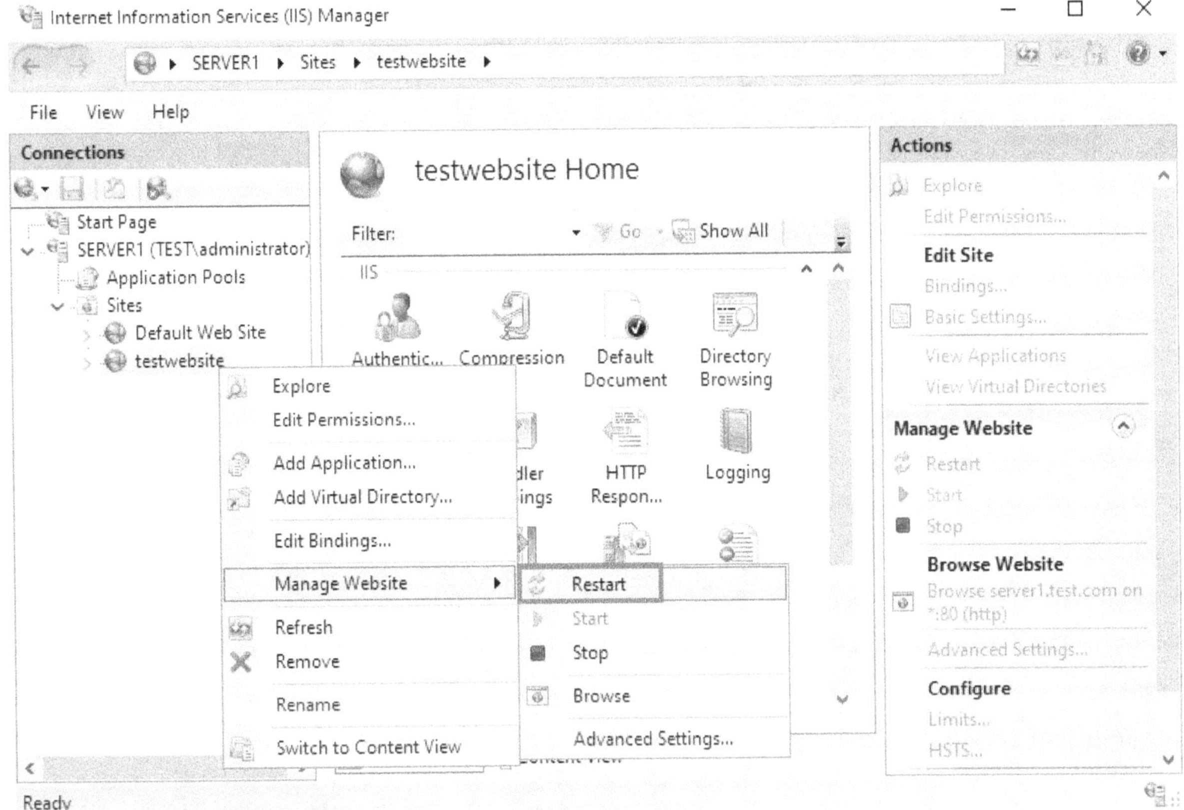

Remove website on IIS Webserver

8. Right click on the Website and Click Remove.

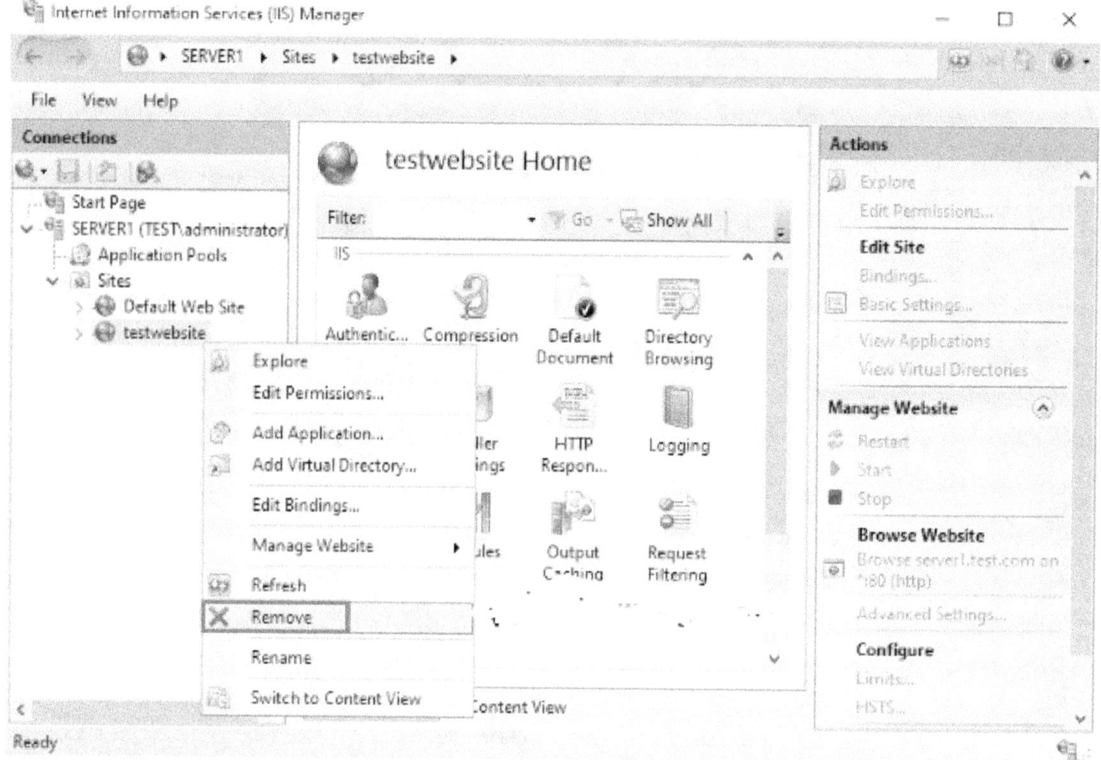

9. Click Yes to Confirm Remove.

9. Click **Yes** to Confirm Remove.

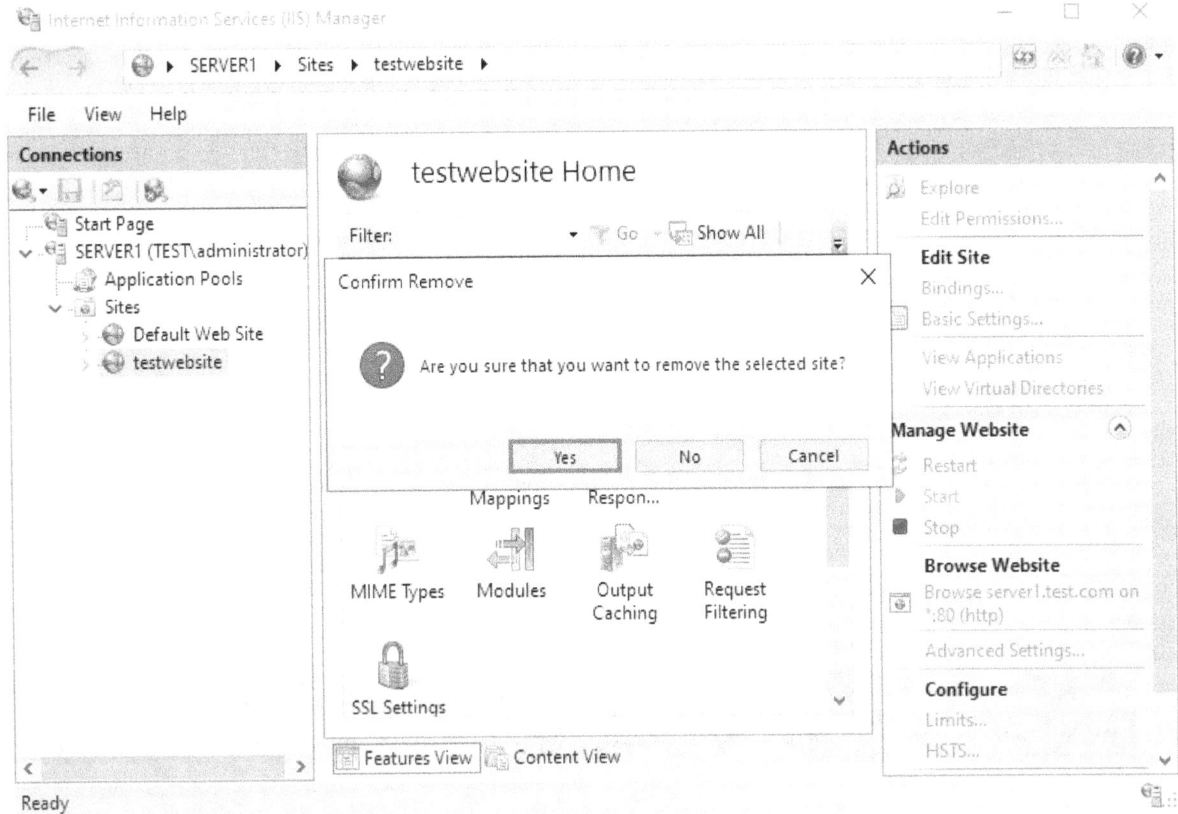

How to set up a file server on Windows Server

Want to create a file share on your Windows Server so that users on your network can transfer to it? Don't know how to set it up? Don't worry; we've got your back! Follow this guide and learn how to set up a file server on <u>Windows Server</u>.

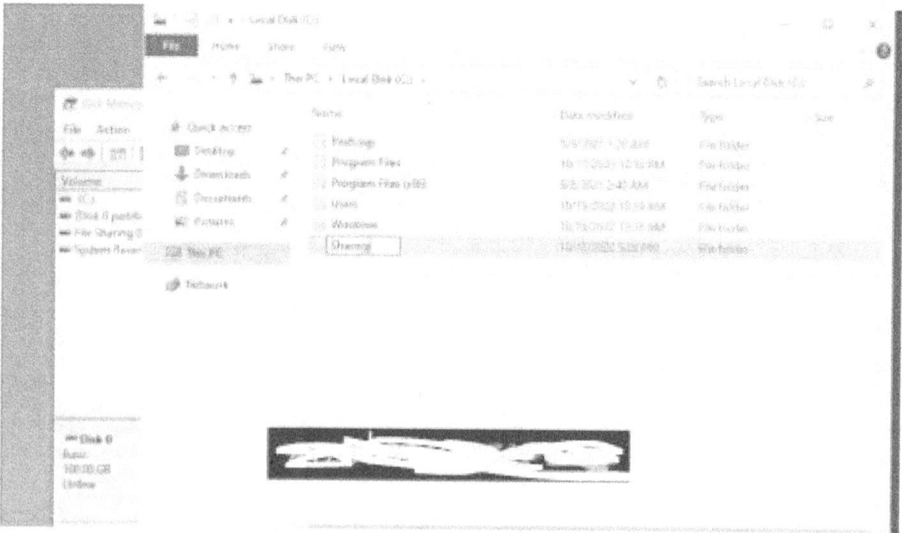

Before we begin

This guide focuses on Windows Server 2022 in GUI mode. If you are using an older release of Windows Server, we highly recommend upgrading to 2022. This tutorial should still work if you do not wish to upgrade, but the UI may differ.

How to create a shared folder on Windows Server

Creating shared folders in Windows Server via the GUI is incredibly easy and similar to how it works on Windows Desktop. To start, launch the Explorer application.

Once the Explorer app is open, find the "This PC" section, and click on it with the mouse. After selecting "This PC," choose either your "Local Disk" (C:) or another drive.

When selecting the hard drive you wish to use for sharing, right-click on an empty space and create a new folder. In this example, we'll create a folder named "Sharing." on the **C:/** root directory.

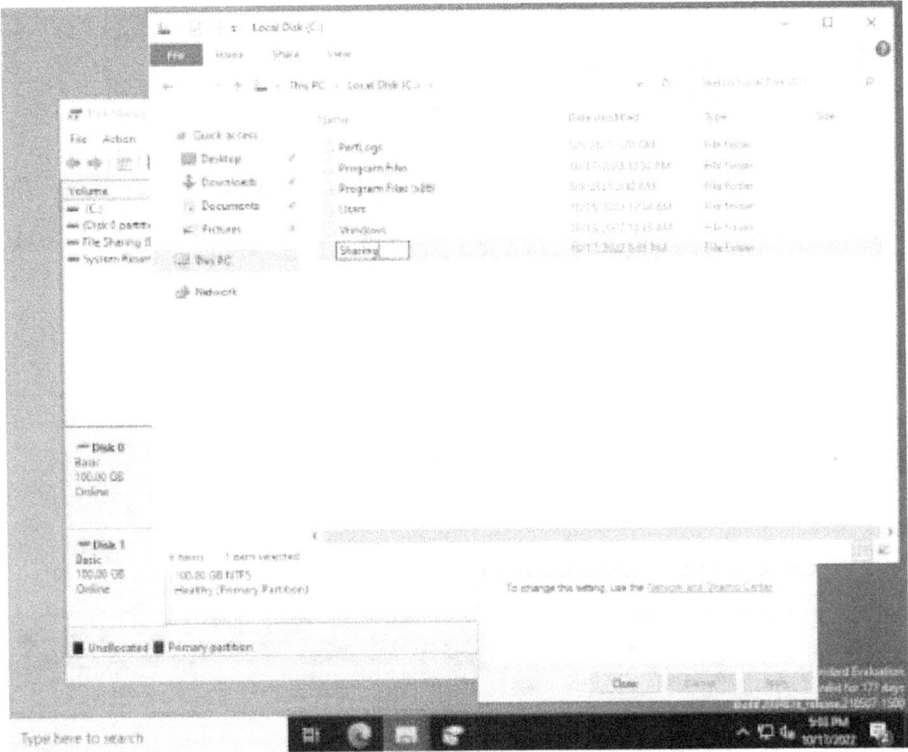

After creating the new "Sharing" folder, right-click on it with the mouse. Then, select the "Properties" option. Selecting "Properties" will open up the "Sharing" folder options.

In the "Properties" window for the "Sharing" folder, select the "Sharing" tab to access the Windows Server share settings for this particular folder. Then, choose the "Advanced Sharing" button.

After clicking on the "Advanced Sharing" button, find the "Share this folder" box, and click on it. Selecting this box will allow the folder to be shared.

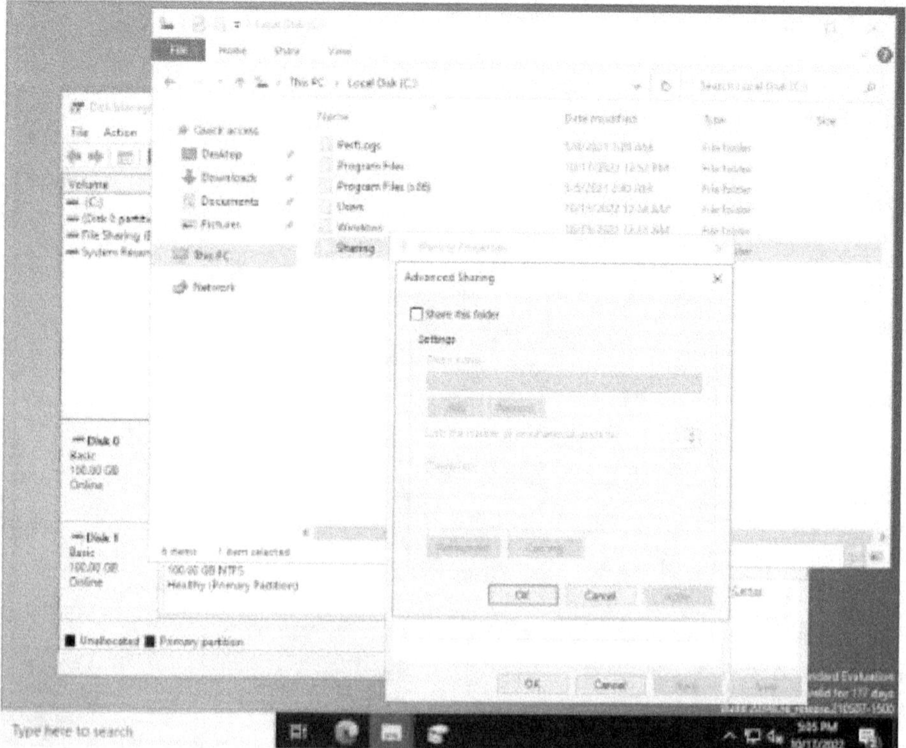

Find the "Comments" section, and enter a brief description of your share. Then, click the "Permissions" button to access the permissions.

Inside the "Permissions" area for the "Sharing" folder, there's a "Share Permissions" tab. Select "Everyone" and change permissions so that "Everyone" has all three boxes checked.

Setting the folder so that "Everyone" can access it means that any user on the Windows Server can read, write, and change things in the shared folder. If you do not want this, you can change it to just "read." Users can only modify files if they log in with an approved account.

Should you add individual accounts to shared folders?

For a home server, it is generally best not to create friction between those trying to access the folder. If you know your server is not pointing to the internet, allowing everyone access to the share without configuring special passwords is safe.

However, if you want your files to be secure, consider only allowing Administrator accounts or accounts you specify in the "Share Permissions" section.

How to share an entire hard drive with Windows Server

It is possible if you'd like to open up a whole hard drive on your Windows Server to the network. To do it, start by opening up the Windows Explorer app. When the Explorer app is open, select "This PC."

In the "This PC" area, locate the hard drive you wish to share and right-click on it with the mouse. After right-clicking on it, select the "Properties" option to open up the settings for the hard drive.

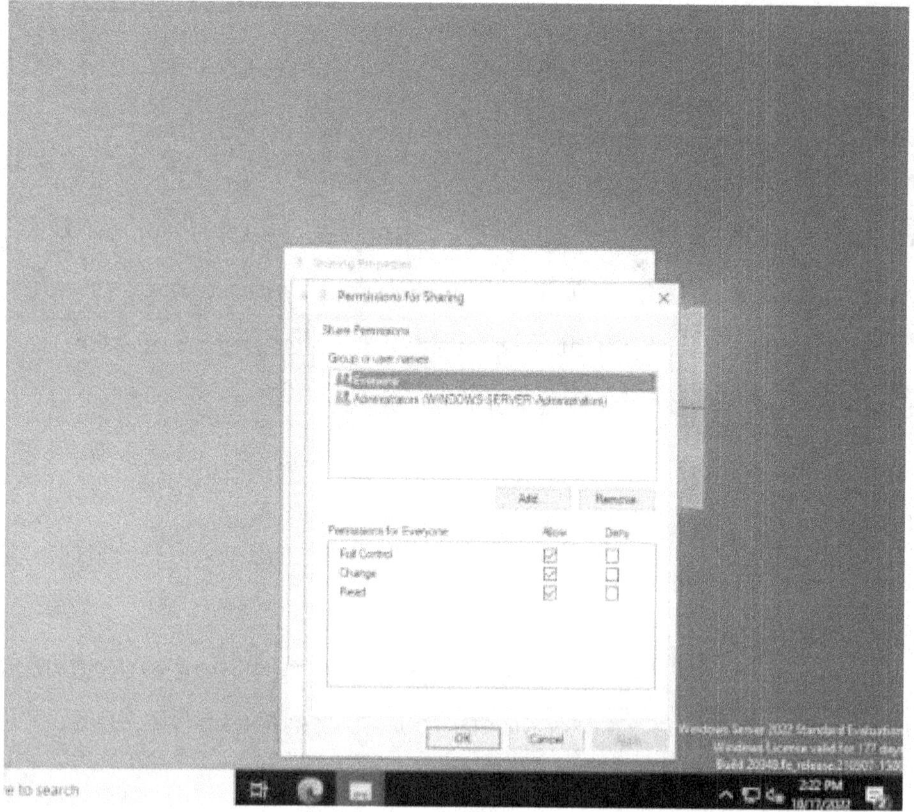

Inside the "Properties" window, choose "Sharing" with the mouse to load up the sharing settings for the drive. Then, select "Share" and configure your sharing settings, permissions, etc. Or, select "Advanced Sharing" if you want more granular control.

How to access the files over the network

Modern operating systems all support the Windows file-sharing protocol (CIFS/Samba). Because of this, it is incredibly easy for anyone on Mac OS, Linux, or Windows to access your server shares.

To access your server shares over the network, do the following. Please note that you must be connected to the same network as the server to access Windows Server shares.

Windows

On a Windows computer, launch Windows Explorer. Then, click on the address bar. Once in the address bar, type in the file server location. In this example, the location is:

\\WINDOWS-SERVER\Files

After entering the address, press the **Enter key** on the keyboard. It should load up the share. If your share requires special permissions, enter it when prompted.

Mac OS/Linux

On Mac OS and Linux, open up the file manager. Once it is open, type the network address with **smb://** in front. For example, to access the Windows server, do the following:

smb://windows-server/Files

CHAPTER 8 : Choosing Server Hardware

The actual computing device we call a server comes in several form factors. The form factor simply defi nes the design of the server's case and internal component access methods. For example, the case may be slim and provide limited component Introducing Servers 7 access or it may be large and bulky with easy component access.

The form factor also dictates how the server may be installed or mounted in the environment. Today, three major form factors exist and are available from many different vendors:

▶ Desktop

▶ Rack Mount

▶ Blade the Desktop form factor looks just like a regular user's client computer. It may be slightly larger, but it will look much the same. The Desktop form factor includes those that stand upright (also known as a tower case) and those that lay horizontal (the traditional Desktop form factor). shows the IBM Power 780 desktop server. While it may appear a little fancier than a regular user's desktop computer, it is essentially the same thing with extra monitoring features and higher quality components.

Figure 1.3 The IBM Power 780
Desktop form factor server

The rack mount servers are specially designed to mount in a rack cabinet. These cabinets typically have doors and are specially ventilated to provide cooling. Figure 1.4 shows the IBM Power 755 rack mount system. To make effi cient use of space, you can mount more than one server in a single rack cabinet. In many scenarios, you can also use a shared uninterruptible power supply (UPS) for all of the servers in the cabinet.

The IBM BladeCenter PS701 Blade form factor server enclosure

The IBM Power 755 Rack Mount form factor server

The final form factor is the server blade. In this case, the server is actually a removable blade that slides into a type of docking station used to house each blade. The docking station (called a BladeCenter by IBM, a Blade Enclosure by Dell, and by other names from other vendors) can house multiple blades. Because each blade is a server, you can store multiple servers in a single docking station. The blade docking station could be a desktop enclosure or it could mount in a rack cabinet, much like a rack server. Figure 1.5 shows the IBM BladeCenter PS701. The form factor you choose will depend on the space in which it will be installed and the number of servers you require.

For example, rack mount and blade servers are very popular when dozens or hundreds of servers are required. When only a few servers are required, the Desktop form factor is still quite common.

Networking Features Windows servers support the popular protocols in use on modern networks. Thanks to the Internet's rapid growth in the 1990s and the fact that it uses the TCP/IP protocol suite, the most popular protocols used today are part of this protocol suite. Windows servers support both the older Internet Protocol (IP) version 4 (IPv4) and the newer IP version 6 (IPv6). The primary difference between the two versions is in their addressing requirements. IPv4 uses a 32-bit (32 ones and zeros) address, and IPv6 uses a 128-bit address for each node on the network. Additional differences exist, but the change in address sizes has the greatest initial impact on organizations moving from IPv4 to IPv6. Windows servers use the TCP/IP protocol suite, as well as other protocols, in order to provide network services.

Built right into the Windows Server operating system is the ability to provide several network services including:

▶ File sharing

▶ Printer sharing

▶ Network authentication

▶ Web serving

▶ Media streaming

▶ Network-based operating system deployments

▶ Network-based operating system update deployments

▶ Network confi guration and resolution services (DHCP and DNS)

▶ Centralized fax services

▶ Data caching services

▶ **Remote command-line services** (Telnet) In addition to these network services, Windows servers can also be used to centrally manage and confi gure Windows clients across the network. A feature known as Group Policy is used to accomplish centralized administration. Using Group Policies on the network, you can deploy software to machines, confi gure operating system settings, and restrict which applications the users can run and much more.

THE ESSENTIALS AND BEYOND *(Continued)*

REVIEW QUESTIONS

1. Which one of the following is the best definition of a server?

   A. A network-connected device that provides IP routing to the network

   B. A network-connected device that provides services to the network and the devices on that network

   C. A stand-alone device that is used by a user to perform mathematical analysis

   D. A network-connected device that is used to access websites using a web browser

2. True or false. SQL Server may be categorized as an information service.

3. What kind of computing device consumes services on a network?

   A. Web Server

   B. DNS Server

   C. Client

   D. Ethernet cable

4. What Command Prompt command can be used to determine the version of Windows running on a machine?

5. Which server form factor allows multiple services to be placed in an enclosure much as add-on cards are installed in individual computers?

   A. Blade

   B. Desktop

   C. Rack Mount

   D. Convertible

6. Define a server role.

7. Define a feature.

8. What server role, in Windows Server 2008 R2, supports centralized scanner management?

   A. File Services

   B. Application Server

   C. Web Server

   D. Print and Document Services

9. What command is used to launch the Windows Command Prompt in Windows Server 2008 R2?

   A. Command.com

   B. PowerShell

   C. CMD

   D. Prompt

10. True or false. Windows Server 2008 R2 supports only IPv4.

How to Install and Configure a Print Server

Print Server is very important roles for the system administrator and the management. Directly All printer sharing via windows server.

This step is requirements in configure time printer management:

- Administrator password must be strong.

- Static IP is configured and windows updates are installed.

- Hardware and Software firewall are turned off.

Installing the Print Server step by step :-

1) Open the **server manager** and Click on the **Add roles and features**.

2)Click on **Next**.

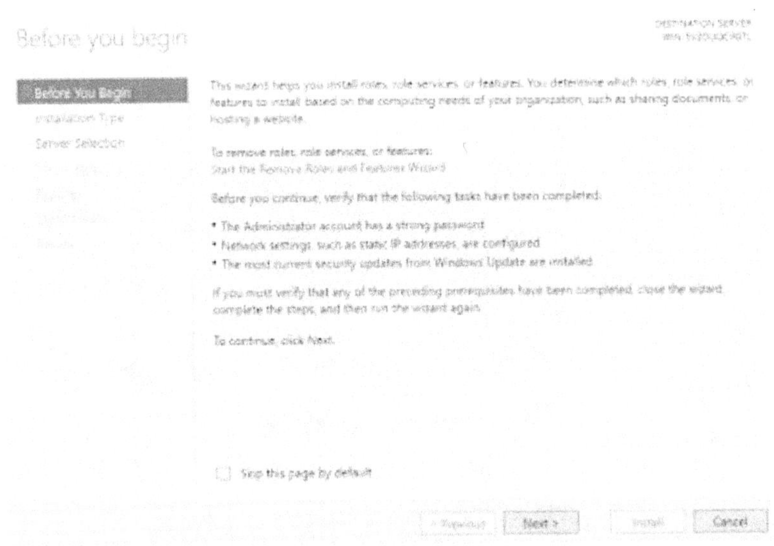

3) Choose **Role-based or feature-based** installation and click on **Next**.

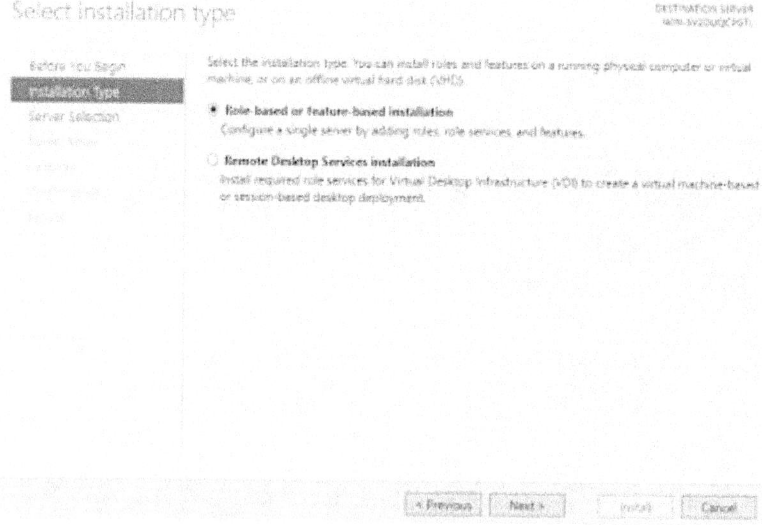

4) Choose the destination printer server for this configuration and click on **Next**.

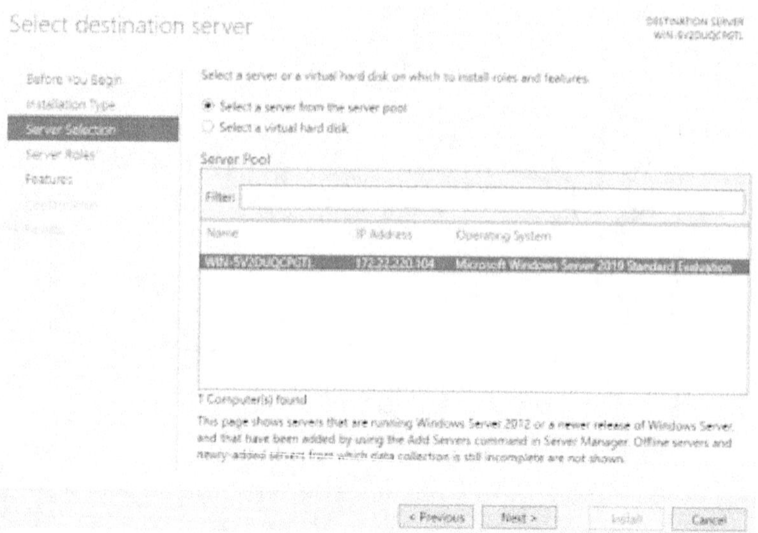

5) Choose the **Print and document services** from server roles and when a new window appear, click on **Add Features**.

6) Click on **Next**.

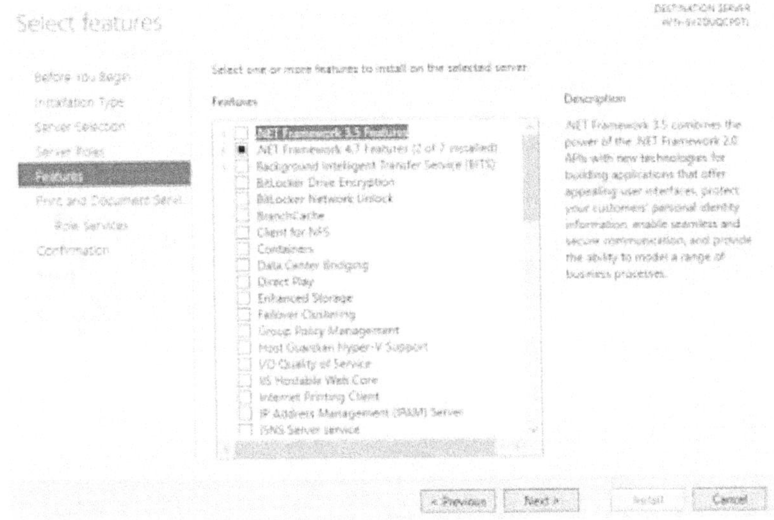

7) Click on **Next**.

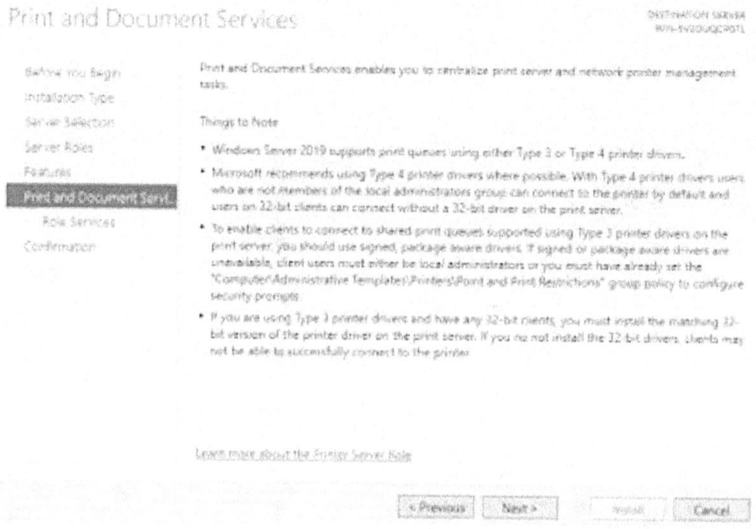

8) Choose **Print Server** and click on **Next**.

9) Click on **Install.**

10) After installation click to **Close** button.

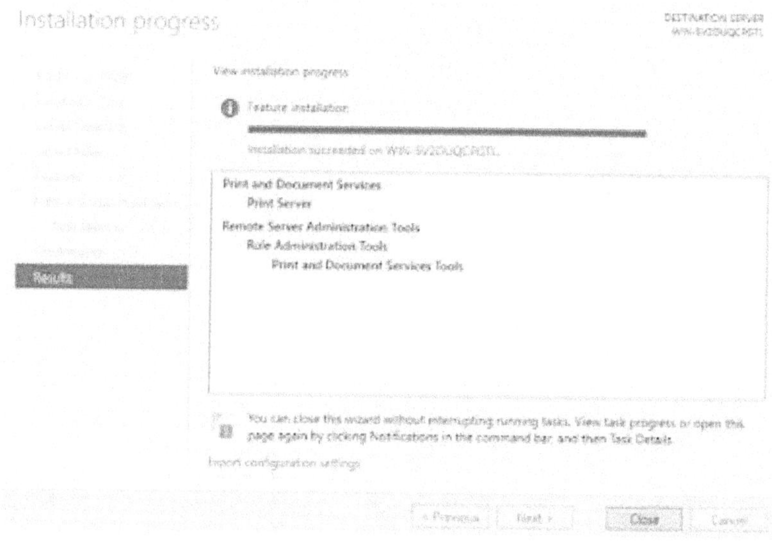

11) Open the **print server management console** in right-click on **Printers server machine** and click on Add Printer. Attach the printer to your infrastructure computer. Choose the right port where your printer is connected.

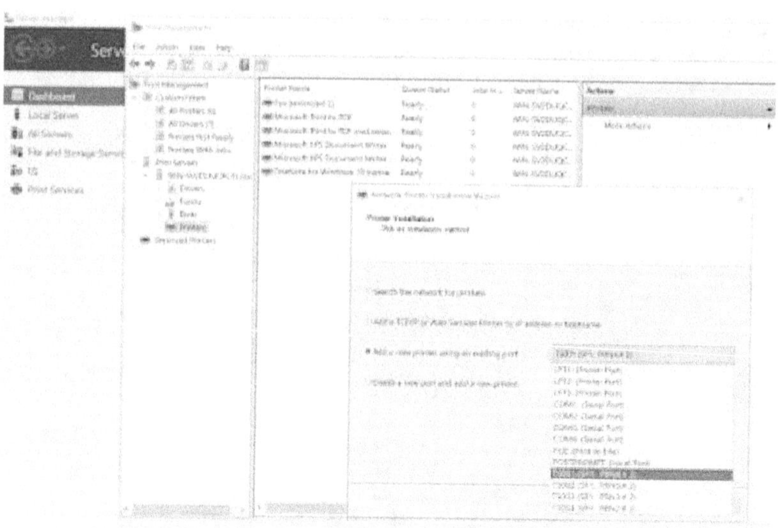

12) Choose the your printer manufacture name and printer model number select.

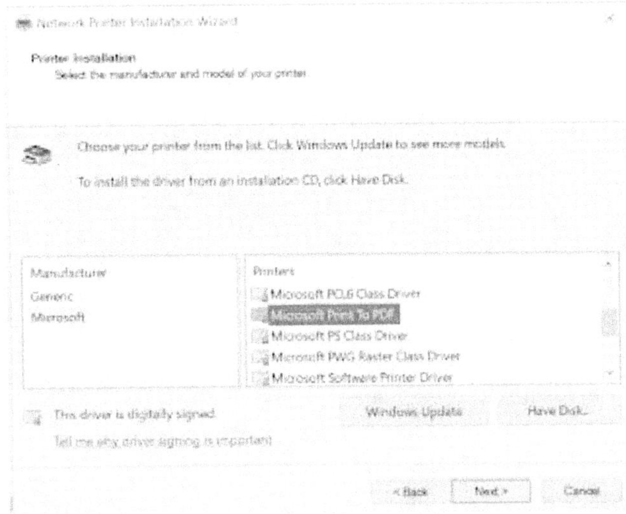

13) Rename the printer name and select the share printer button.

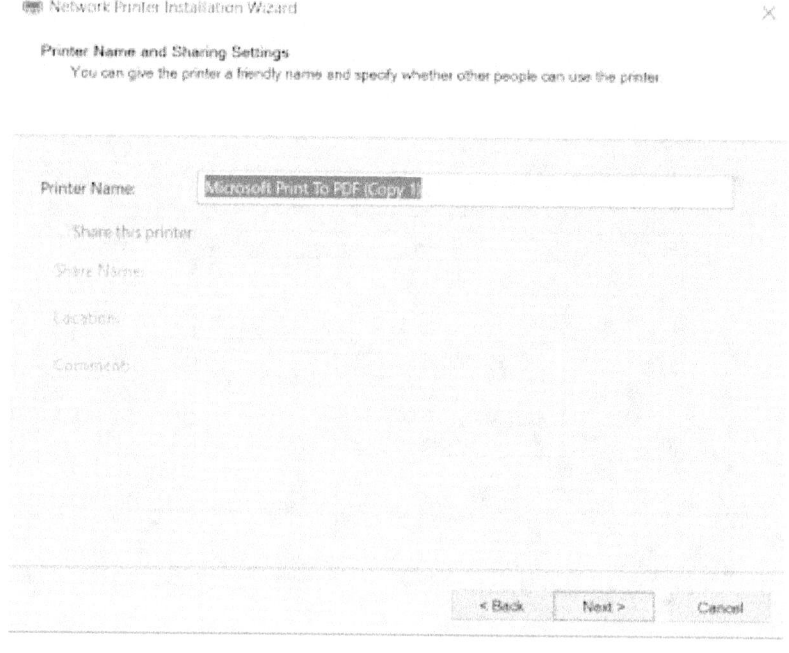

14) Click on **Finish** button.

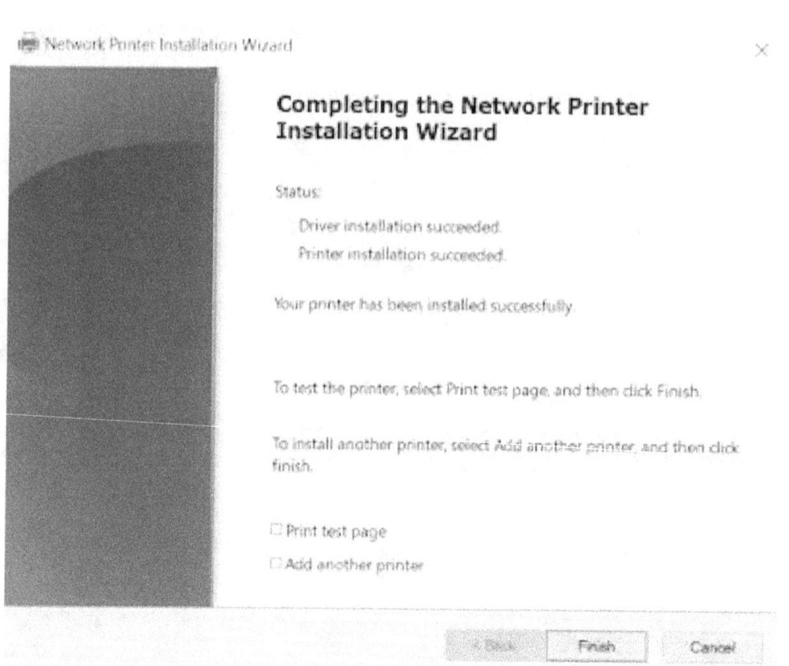

You have successfully configured and deployed your network print server. This printer will be visible to other users on your infrastructure network.

CHAPTER 9 : Install and Configure MySQL on a Windows Server 2022

In this book, we'll take a gander at how you can install and configure MySQL on a Windows server 2022 in merely two simple steps. MySQL server is offered in two editions: an open-source MySQL community server edition and an enterprise server edition. We will be using **the community server for the tutorial**. Let's begin!

Step 1 –

Download MySQL for your Windows Server 2022

The first step to install and configure MySQL on a Windows Server 2022 is to download the MySQL community server from its official website. You can download MySQL for Windows directly from MySQL.com.

The "MySQL Community Server" edition is free and available for both 32-bit (x86) and 64-bit (x64) operating systems.

Hence, download MySQL for your Windows server 2022 depending upon whether your server runs a 32 or 64-bit Windows operating system. Note that the installer for either version is 32-bit only.

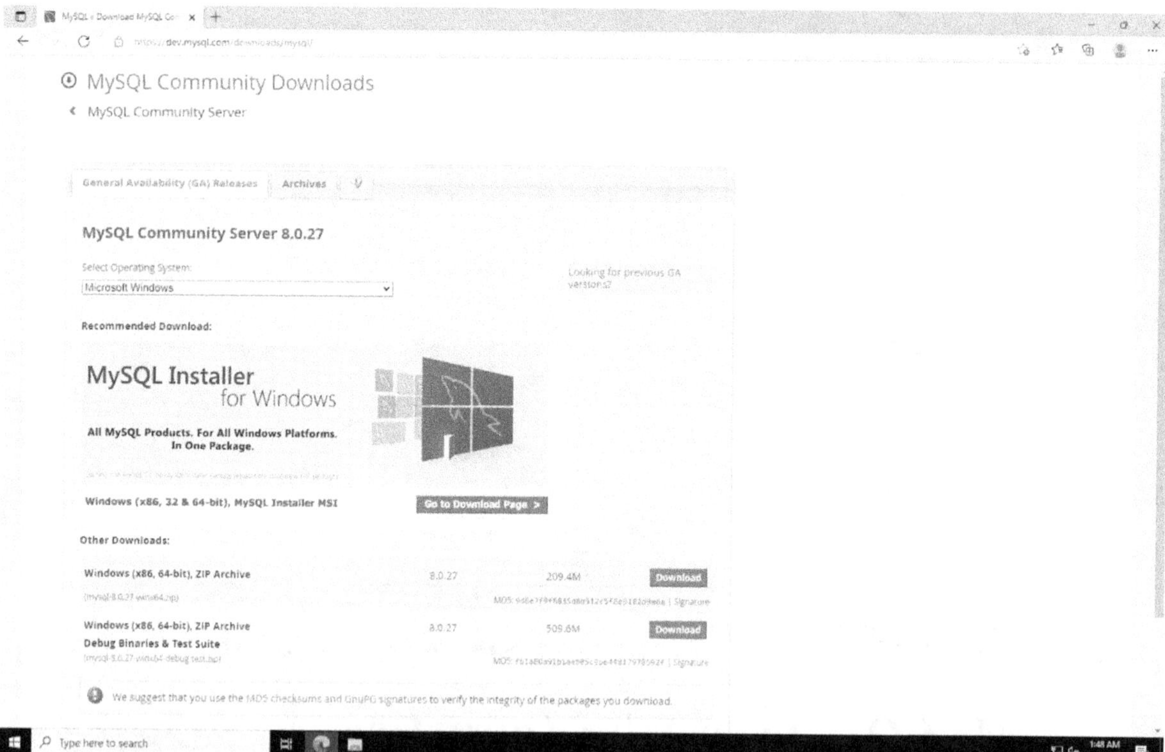

The MySQL Community Server installer is available in both web-installer and standalone-installer modes. Hit "**Download**" after choosing the suitable version of the installer.

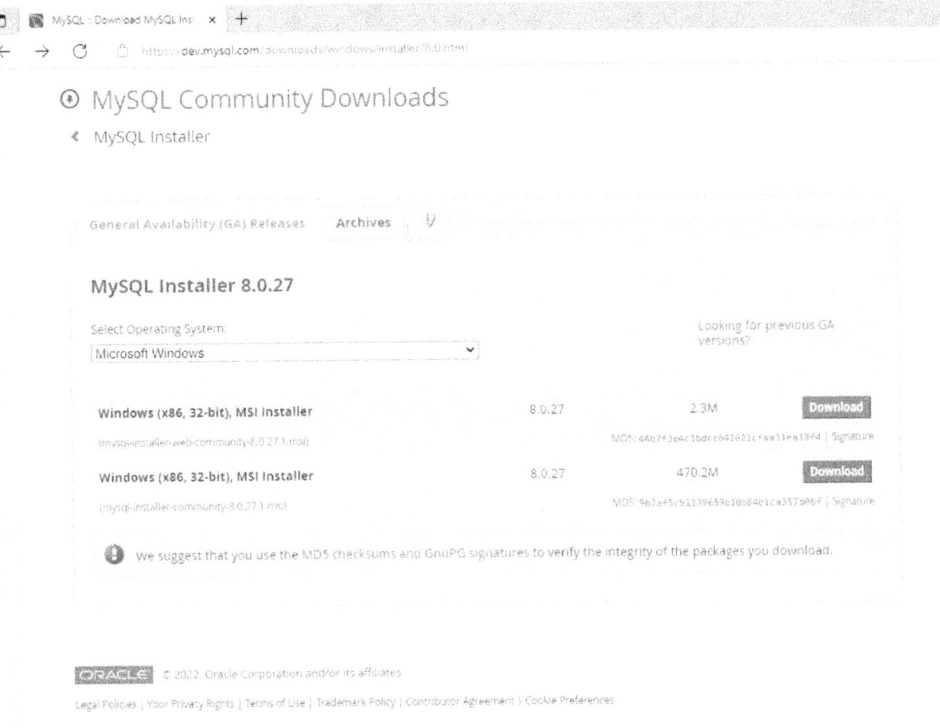

You will then see the option to sign up or log in to an Oracle Web account. However, you can just click on the "*No thanks just start my download*" link.

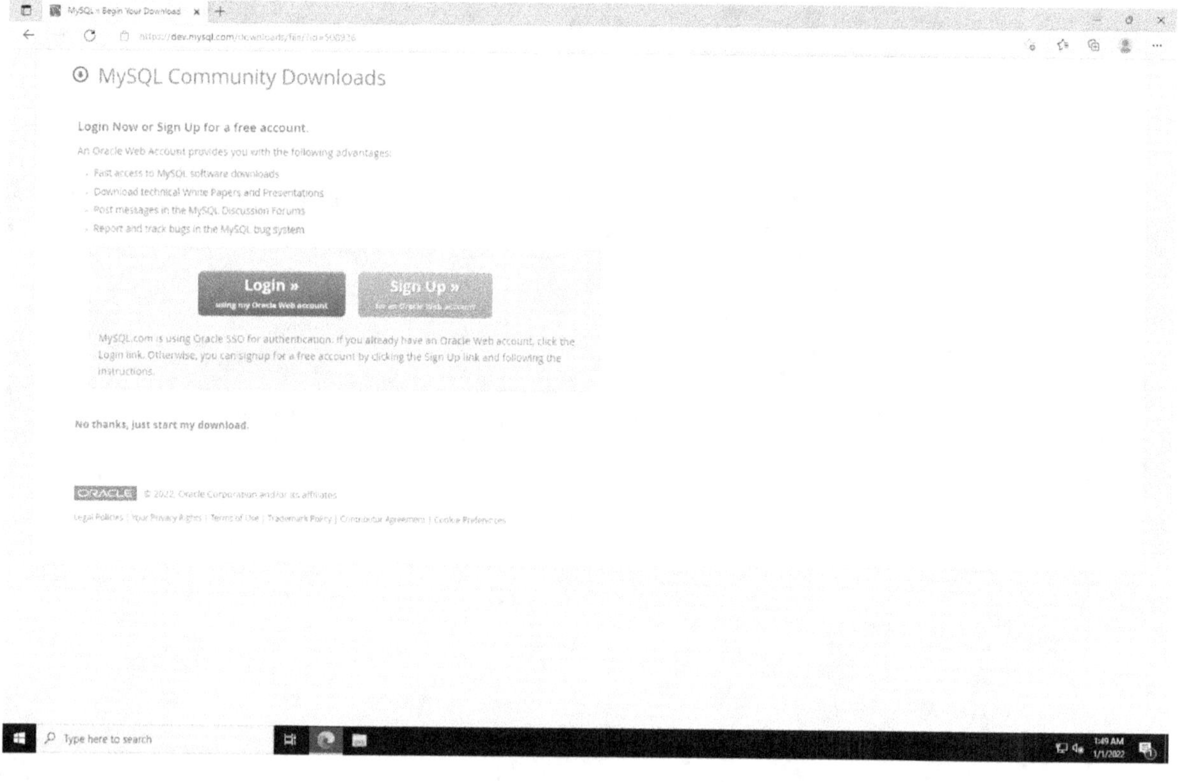

Step 2 –

Install MySQL Community Server on your Windows 2022 Server
Start the installation process by running the MySQL Installer file. You will see the **License Agreement**. We recommend you to read it thoroughly and accept it.

Then you'll be asked to choose a setup type. Since our goal is to configure MySQL on your Windows server 2022, we will go with "**Server only**". Also, as a minimum, you need to install the MySQL server.

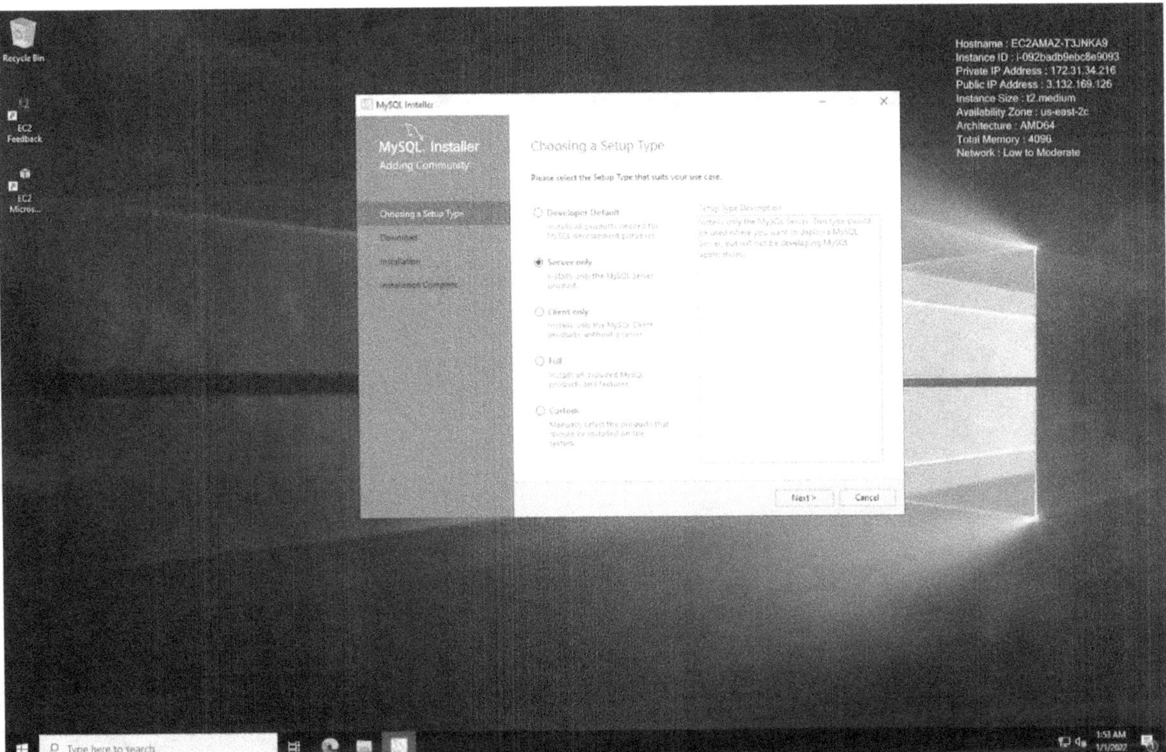

If you had downloaded a standalone web installer, the selected components will start getting installed. In the case of a web installer, the installer will first download the components and then install them.

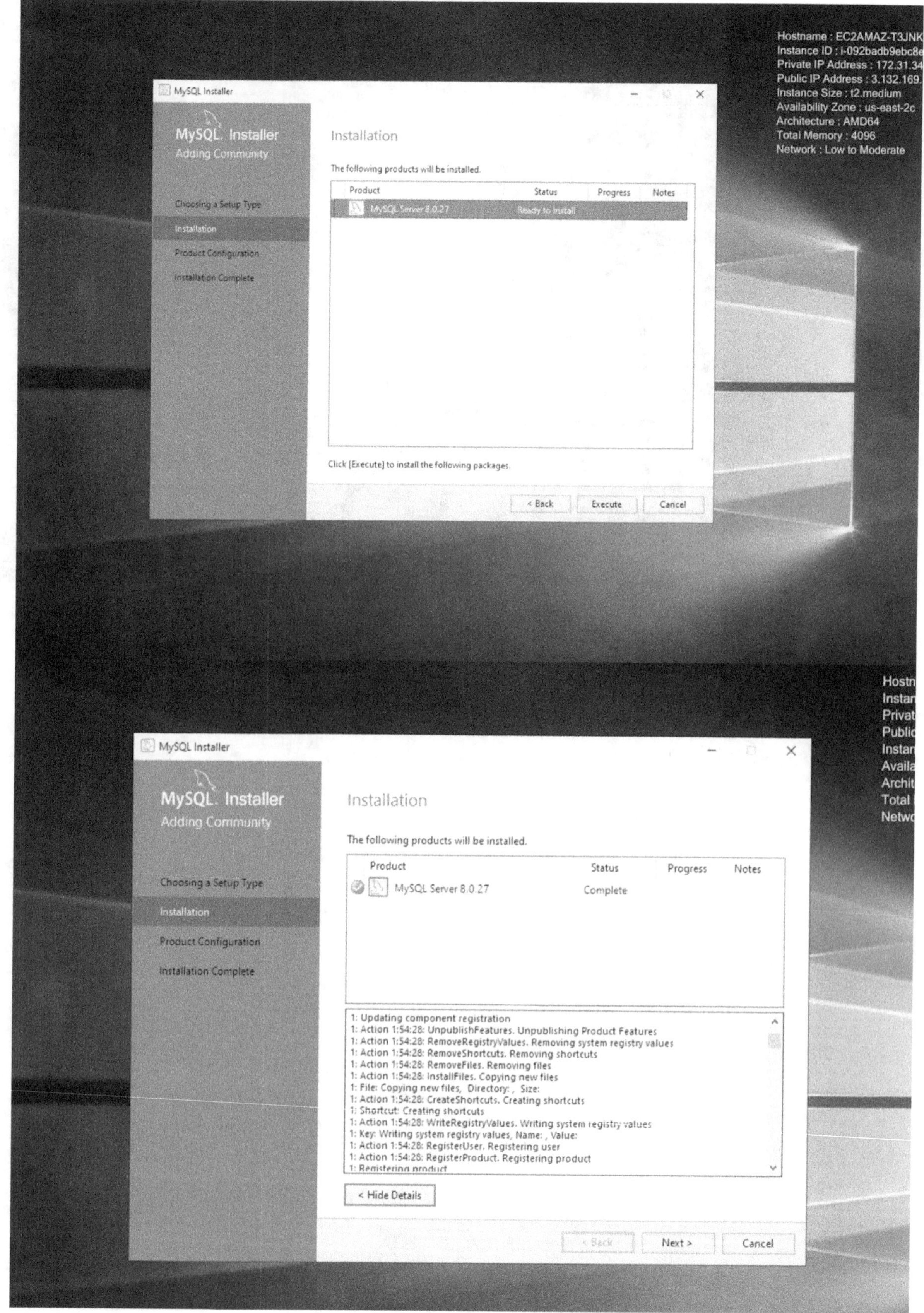

Now that all the necessary components for setting up MySQL on a Windows server 2022 are installed, let's get down to configuration.

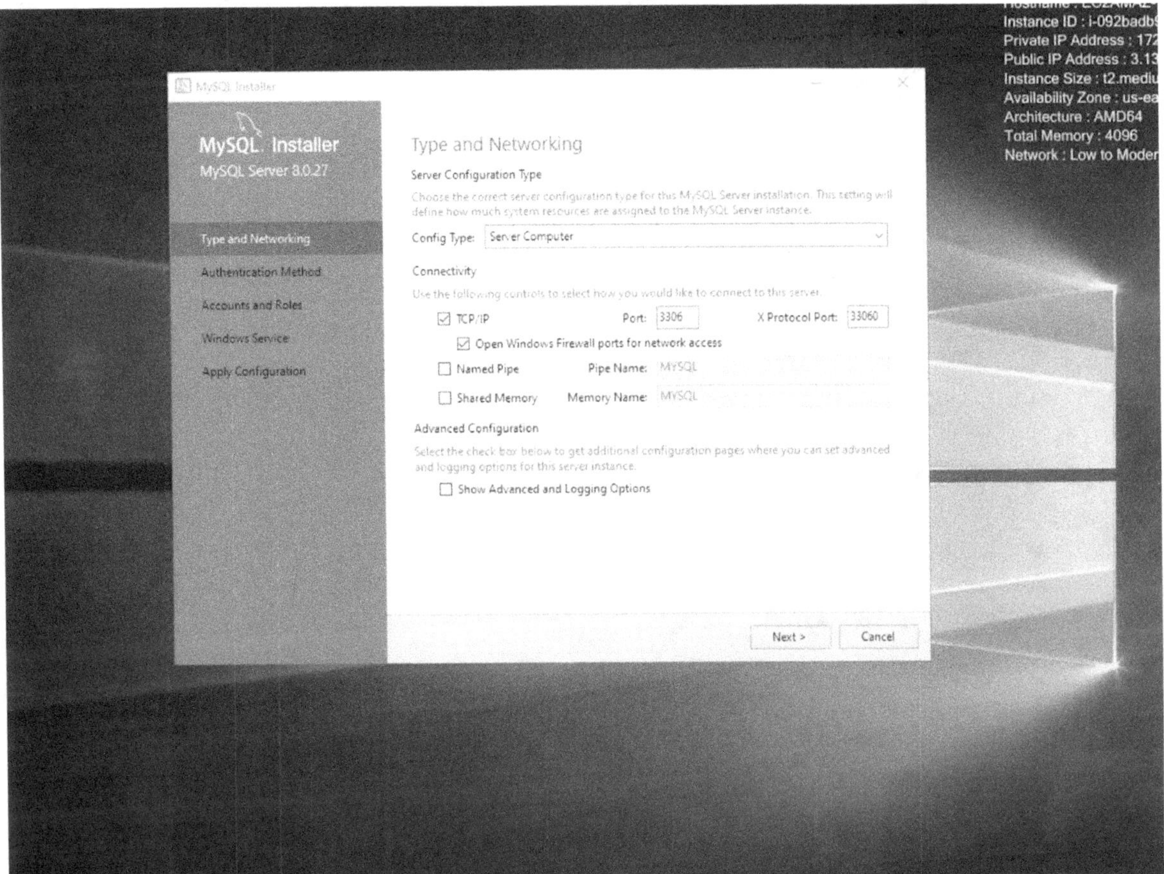

Configuring the MySQL server on your Windows 2022 server is extremely simple. First, you need to select the "**Config Type**" or Configuration Type. Select the configuration type which is most applicable to your server. If you're configuring MySQL on your Windows 2022 server where other applications are installed/running, select "*Server Machine*". Select "*Dedicated Machine*" if the server will just be dedicated to MySQL and won't be running any other applications/services.

In addition, you can configure the server for specific "*Connectivity*" options. However, you can leave the default configuration(TCP/IP Port 3306) in most cases.

Hit the "**Next**" button to proceed. You should now be prompted to set up a MySQL root password:

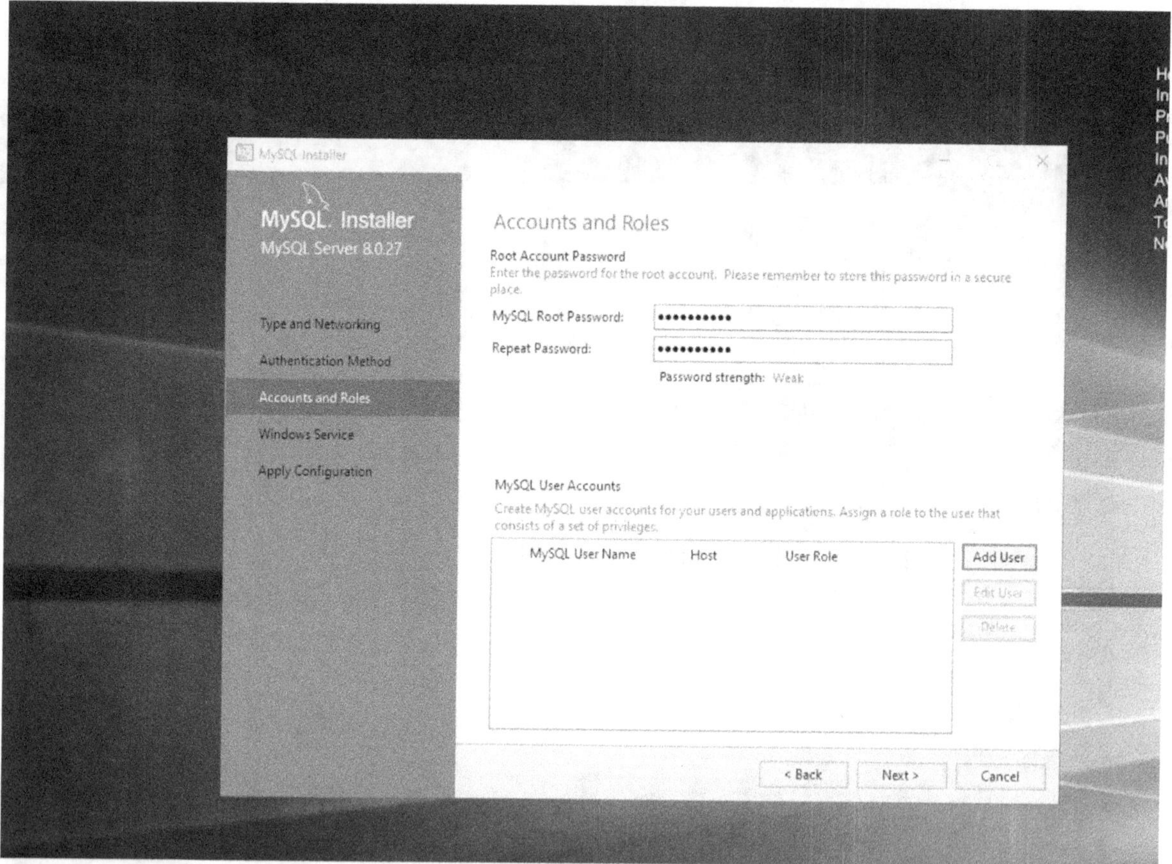

The MySQL root password protects your MySQL server from unauthorized changes/access. Hence, it should be a strong and secure password. In addition, you can also add additional MySQL user accounts on this step. The whole idea behind setting up dedicated MySQL user accounts for each service is to configure the server to be used for multiple applications as well as MIDAS.

Then, Hit "**Next**" and you will see the options to configure MySQL as a Windows Service. This would mean that the server will run automatically whenever Windows starts:

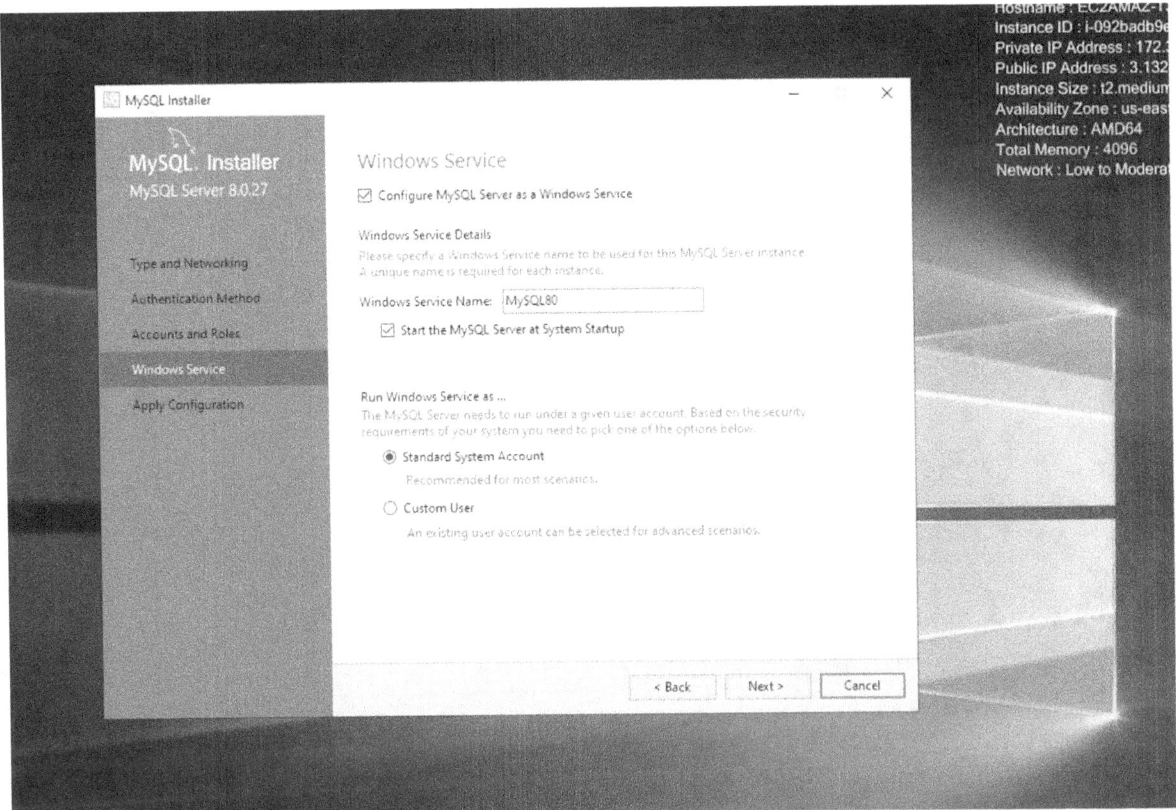

Check the "**Configure MySQL Server as a Windows Service**" and "**Start the MySQL Server at System Startup**" checkboxes. Finally, select the "**Standard System Account**" radio button.

Finally, click "**Next**" and you will have configured MySQL on a Windows server 2022 successfully.

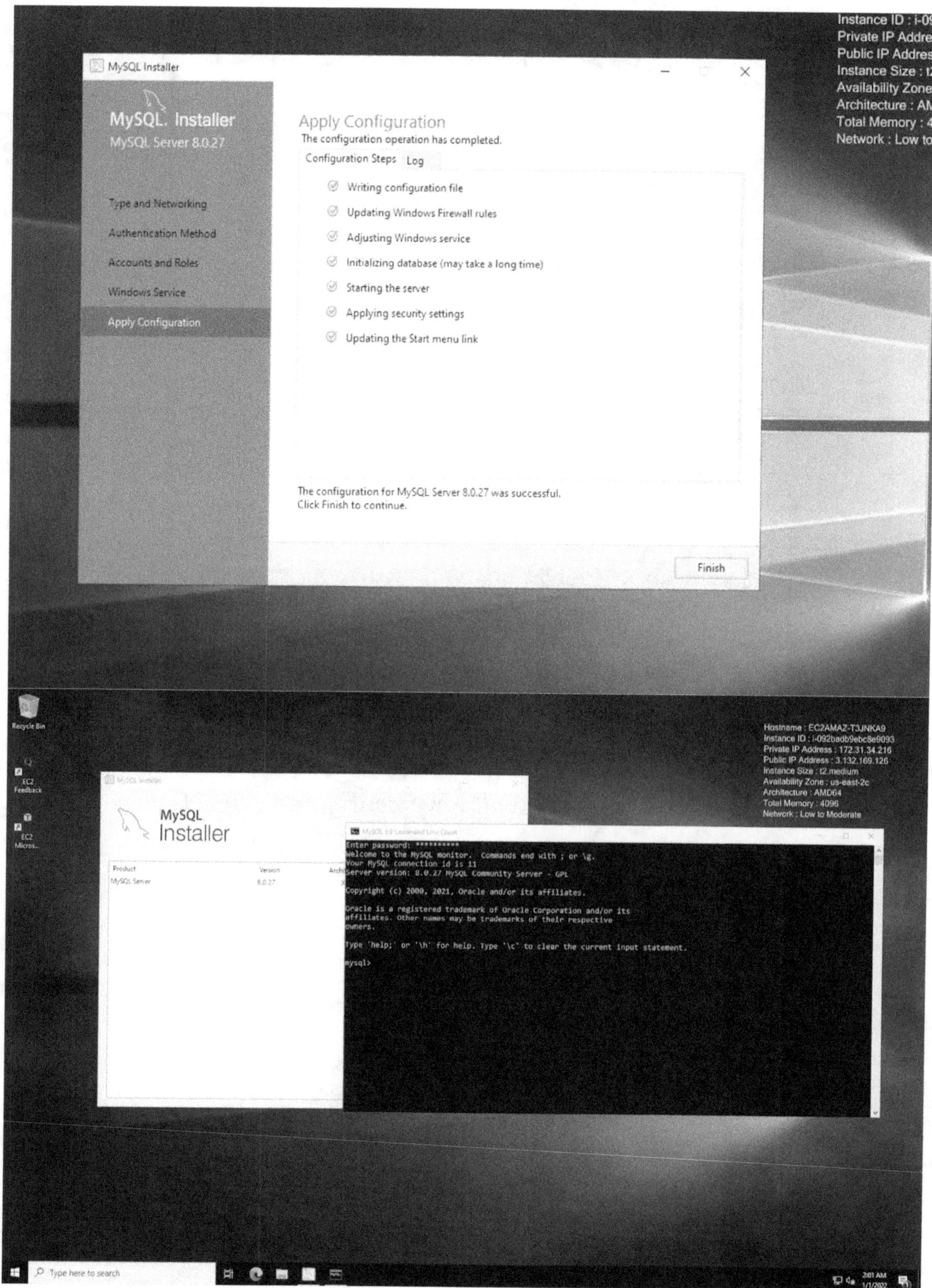

Windows Server Glossary

This glossary explains the meaning of key words and phrases that information technology (IT) and business professionals use when discussing Microsoft Windows Server and related software products.

Microsoft Technology Associate (MTA) certification

Microsoft Technology Associate (MTA) certification is the name of a suite of entry-level certifications offered by Microsoft that signify fundamental technology knowledge in those who earn it.

- 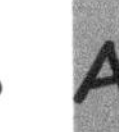 A

active directory

Active Directory (AD) is Microsoft's proprietary directory service.

- ### Active Directory domain (AD domain)

  An Active Directory domain (AD domain) is a collection of objects within a Microsoft Active Directory network.

- ### Active Directory forest (AD forest)

  An Active Directory forest is the highest level of organization within Active Directory.

- ### Active Directory functional levels

  Active Directory functional levels are controls that specify which advanced Active Directory domain features can be used in an enterprise domain.

- <u>Active Directory tree</u>

  An Active Directory (AD) tree is a collection of domains within a Microsoft Active Directory network.

- <u>Azure DevOps</u>

  Azure DevOps -- rebranded from Visual Studio Team Services (VSTS) in 2018 -- is a software-as-a service (SaaS) platform from Microsoft designed to provide a comprehensive toolchain for developing and deploying software projects.

- 

  <u>backup domain controller (Windows NT)</u>

  A backup domain controller (BDC) is a role a Windows NT computer takes on to help manage access to network resources.

- <u>batch file</u>

  A batch file is a script file that stores commands to be executed in a serial order.

- <u>blue screen of death (BSOD)</u>

  Officially called the stop screen, or stop error, the blue screen of death (BSOD) is a most unwanted error, second only to malware or ransomware in indicating that a user is in for a very bad day.

- <u>boot</u>

  To boot (to boot up, to start up or booting) a computer is to load an operating system (OS) into the computer's main memory or random-access memory (RAM).

- <u>built-in administrator account</u>

  In the Windows operating system, the built-in administrator account -- the first account created when the OS was installed -- has the highest permissions of any profile on the computer system.

- C

  <u>C</u>

  The C programming language is a procedural and general-purpose language that provides low-level access to system memory.

- <u>canonical name (CNAME)</u>

  A canonical name (CNAME) is a type of Domain Name System (DNS) database record that indicates that a domain name is the nickname or alias for another domain name.

- <u>CHKDSK (check disk)</u>

  CHKDSK (pronounced check disk) is a command that displays a status report for a volume, such as a disk, and can correct any errors found in that volume.

- <u>Client Access Server (CAS)</u>

  The Client Access Server (CAS) is a server role that handles all client connections to Exchange Server 2010 and Exchange 2013.

- <u>client-server network</u>

  A client-server network is a communications model in which multiple client programs share the services of a common server program.

- <u>CNAME</u>

  A CNAME specifies an alias or nickname for a canonical name record in a domain name system (DNS) database. (Continued...)

- <u>cold/warm/hot server</u>

  In the backup and recovery of a computer server, a cold server is a backup server whose purpose is solely to be there in case the main server is lost.

- <u>command-line interface (CLI)</u>

  A command-line interface (CLI) is a text-based user interface (UI) used to run programs, manage computer files and interact with the computer.

- <u>computer</u>

  A computer is a device that accepts information (in the form of digitalized data) and manipulates it for some result based on a program, software, or sequence of instructions on how the data is to be processed.

- <u>configuration drift</u>

  Configuration drift occurs naturally in data center environments when changes to software and hardware are not recorded or tracked in a comprehensive and systematic fashion.

- <u>CSV (Cluster Shared Volumes)</u>

  CSV (Cluster Shared Volumes) is a feature in Windows Server in which shared disks are concurrently accessible to all nodes within a failover cluster.

- <u>Ctrl-Alt-Delete</u>

  On a personal computer with the Microsoft Windows operating system, Control+Alt+Delete is the combination of the Ctrl key, the Alt key, and Del key that a user can press at the same time to terminate an application task or to reboot the operating system.

- 

  <u>defragmentation</u>

  Defragmentation is the process of locating the noncontiguous fragments of data into which a computer file may be divided as it is stored on a hard disk, and rearranging the fragments and restoring them into fewer fragments or into the whole file.

- <u>Directory Services Restore Mode (DSRM)</u>

  Directory Services Restore Mode (DSRM) is a Safe Mode boot option for Windows Server domain controllers.

- <u>diskpart (Disk Partition Utility)</u>

  Diskpart is a command line utility in Windows operating systems (OSs) that is used to manage disks, partitions, and volumes.

- <u>domain controller</u>

  A domain controller is a type of server that processes requests for authentication from users within a computer domain.

- <u>dynamic link library (DLL)</u>

  A dynamic link library (DLL) is a collection of small programs that larger programs can load when needed to complete specific tasks.

- 

Exchange Administration Center (EAC)

The Exchange Administration Center (EAC) is a Web-based management console for managing Exchange Server 2013 environments.

- Exchange Autodiscover service

The Exchange Autodiscover service helps Exchange administrators set up and sustain server settings for computers that run Microsoft Outlook, as well as settings for supported mobile devices.

- Exchange Management Console (EMC)

The Exchange Management Console (EMC), introduced by Microsoft in 2007, is an administrative tool with a graphical user interface (GUI) that's used to manage the components and resources of Microsoft Exchange Server.

- Exchange Online

Exchange Online is the hosted version of Microsoft's Exchange Server messaging platform that organizations can obtain as a stand-alone service or via an Office 365 subscription.

- Exchange staged migration

The staged Exchange migration process transfers data and mailboxes from one Exchange server to another, either on-premises or in the cloud.

- Exchange Web Services (EWS)
Microsoft Exchange Web Services (EWS) is an application program interface (API) that lets applications access items in a Microsoft Exchange email mailbox, such as calendars, contacts, and messages.

- 

failover cluster
In computing, a failover cluster refers to a group of independent servers that work together to maintain high availability of applications and services.

- 

global catalog (Active Directory)
A global catalog is a data storage source containing partial representations of objects found in a multi-domain Active Directory Domain Services forest.

- <u>gpresult</u>

    Gpresult is a command-line tool that shows the RSoP (Resultant Set of Policy) for a user or computer based on applied Group Policy settings.

- <u>Group Policy</u>

    Group Policy is a hierarchical infrastructure that allows a network administrator in charge of Microsoft's Active Directory to implement specific configurations for users and computers. Group policy is primarily a security tool, and can be used to apply security settings to users and computers.

- <u>Group Policy Editor (GP Editor)</u>

    Group Policy Editor is a tool that helps administrators manage policy settings in Microsoft Management Console (MMC) snap-ins.

- <u>Group Policy Management Console (GPMC)</u>

    Group Policy Management Console (GPMC) is a Microsoft Management Console snap-in that provides a graphical user interface that enables Active Directory (AD) administrators to manage Group Policy Objects (GPOs) from one console.

- <u>Group Policy Object (GPO)</u>

    Microsoft's Group Policy Object (GPO) is a collection of Group Policy settings that defines what a system will look like and how it will behave for a defined group of users.

- <u>Group Policy Preferences</u>

    Group Policy Preferences are a set of extensions, introduced in Windows Server 2008, that increase the functionality of Group Policy Objects.

- <u>GUID (global unique identifier)</u>
    A GUID (globally unique identifier) is a 128-bit text string that represents an identification (ID).

- 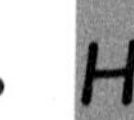 **H**

    <u>hotfix</u>
    A hotfix is code -- sometimes called a patch -- that fixes a bug in a product.

- **I**

<u>Internet Information Services (IIS)</u>
Internet Information Services (IIS) is a flexible, general-purpose web server from Microsoft that runs on Windows systems to serve requested HTML pages or files.

- <u>ISA (Industry Standard Architecture)</u>

  ISA (Industry Standard Architecture) is a standard bus (computer interconnection) architecture that was associated with the IBM AT motherboard.

- 

<u>Linux Secure Boot</u>
Linux Secure Boot is a feature in Windows 10 and Windows Server 2016 that allows some Linux distributions to boot under Hyper-V as Generation 2 virtual machines.

- <u>Local Group Policy Editor</u>
  Local Group Policy Editor is a Microsoft Management Console (MMC) snap-in that provides a user interface for managing local Group Policy settings on a Windows computer.

- 

<u>Active Directory Domain Services (AD DS)</u>
Active Directory Domain Services (AD DS) is a server role in Active Directory that allows admins to manage and store information about resources from a network, as well as application data, in a distributed database.

- <u>MCITP (Microsoft Certified IT Professional)</u>

  An MCITP (Microsoft Certified IT Professional) is a credential that proves that an individual has a complete set of skills required to perform a particular IT job role, such as enterprise or virtualization administrator.

- <u>Microsoft</u>

  Microsoft is the largest vendor of computer software in the world.

- <u>Microsoft Active Directory Migration Tool (ADMT)</u>

  The Microsoft Active Directory Migration Tool (ADMT) is a free utility administrators can use to move Active Directory objects, such as computers, users and groups, from one Windows Server Active Directory domain or forest to another.

- <u>Microsoft AzMan (Microsoft Authorization Manager)</u>

  Microsoft AzMan (Authorization Manager) is a role-based access and security framework for .NET applications.

- <u>Microsoft Azure ExpressRoute</u>

  Microsoft Azure ExpressRoute is a service that provides a private connection between an organization's on-premises infrastructure and Microsoft Azure data centers.

- <u>Microsoft Azure File Service</u>

  Microsoft Azure File Service is a service that allows Windows Server admins to access SMB shares in the Azure cloud by setting up file shares in the Azure management console.

- <u>Microsoft Azure Key Vault</u>

  Microsoft Azure Key Vault is a cloud-based security service offered by Microsoft as part of its Azure platform.

- <u>Microsoft Azure Stack</u>

  Microsoft Azure Stack is an integrated platform of hardware and software that delivers Microsoft Azure public cloud services in a local data center to enable organizations to construct hybrid clouds.

- <u>Microsoft Certified Systems Engineer (MCSE)</u>

  The Microsoft Certified Systems Engineer (MCSE) is a certification that was offered by Microsoft for IT professionals who demonstrated expertise in designing, implementing, and administering Windows server infrastructure, as well as other Microsoft technologies.

- <u>Microsoft Cloud Witness</u>

  Microsoft Cloud Witness is a quorum witness for Windows Server Failover Clustering (WSFC) that uses Microsoft Azure as the arbitration point.

- <u>Microsoft Cluster Service (MSCS)</u>

  Microsoft Cluster Service (MSCS) is a service that provides high availability (HA) for applications such as databases, messaging and file and print services.

- <u>Microsoft Connectivity Analyzer (MCA)</u>

  The Microsoft Connectivity Analyzer (MCA) is a diagnostics tool for troubleshooting and testing connectivity to several Microsoft messaging products from a client machine on an organization's network.

- <u>Microsoft Exchange Control Panel</u>

  The Exchange Control Panel (ECP) is a Web-based management interface introduced in Exchange Server 2010.

- <u>Microsoft Exchange In-Place eDiscovery</u>

  Microsoft Exchange In-Place eDiscovery is an administrative feature to perform legal discovery searches for relevant content in mailboxes.

- <u>Microsoft Exchange Mailbox Replication Service (MRS)</u>

  The Microsoft Exchange Mailbox Replication Service (MRS) is a feature that handles mailbox import, export, migration and restoration requests on Exchange Server.

- <u>Microsoft Exchange Management Shell (EMS)</u>

  Microsoft Exchange Management Shell (EMS) is a scripting platform that enables administrators to manage Exchange Server. EMS is is built on top of Microsoft PowerShell, a command line shell that allows administrators to perform administrative tasks with simple noun-verb commands called cmdlets.

- <u>Microsoft Exchange Online Protection (EOP)</u>

  Microsoft Exchange Online Protection (EOP) is a cloud-based service that provides email filtering designed to protect organizations against spam, malware, and other email-based threats.

- <u>Microsoft Exchange RBAC (Role Based Access Control)</u>

  Microsoft Exchange RBAC is a permissions model used in Exchange Server 2010 and Exchange Server 2013.

- <u>Microsoft Exchange Server</u>

  Microsoft Exchange Server is Microsoft's email, calendaring, contact, scheduling and collaboration platform.

- <u>Microsoft Exchange Server 2016</u>

  Microsoft Exchange Server 2016 is the latest iteration of the Exchange Server messaging platform. It is tentatively scheduled for release in the latter half of 2015.

- <u>Microsoft Failover Cluster Manager (MSFCM)</u>

  Microsoft Failover Cluster Manager (MSFCM) is a specific management function within the Windows Server operating system which is used to create, validate, and manage failover server clusters running Windows Server.

- <u>Microsoft Group Policy administrative template</u>

  A Microsoft Group Policy administrative template is a file that supports the implementation of Microsoft Windows Group Policy and centralized user and machine management in Active Directory environments.

- <u>Microsoft Hybrid Configuration Wizard</u>

  The Microsoft Hybrid Configuration Wizard (HCW) is a tool provided by Microsoft to help organizations set up and configure a hybrid deployment between their on-premises Exchange Server and Exchange Online, which is part of Microsoft 365.

- <u>Microsoft Hyper-V Manager</u>

  Microsoft Hyper-V Manager is a tool that allows administrators to create, change and delete virtual machines (VMs).

- <u>Microsoft Hyper-V Shielded VM</u>

  A Microsoft Hyper-V Shielded VM is a security feature of Windows Server 2016 that protects a Hyper-V second-generation virtual machine (VM) from access or tampering by using a combination of Secure Boot, BitLocker encryption, virtual Trusted Platform Module (TPM) and the Host Guardian Service.

- <u>Microsoft Identity Manager</u>

  Microsoft Identity Manager -- also called Microsoft Identity Manager 2016 or MIM -- is an on-premises tool that enables organizations to manage access, users, policies and credentials.

- <u>Microsoft iSCSI Initiator</u>

  Microsoft iSCSI Initiator is a tool that connects external iSCSI-based storage to host computers with an Ethernet network adapter.

- <u>Microsoft Log Parser Studio</u>

  Microsoft Log Parser Studio is a front-end utility that features a graphical user interface, report builder and query repository for Microsoft's Log Parser application.

- <u>Microsoft Monitoring Agent (MMA)</u>

  Microsoft Monitoring Agent (MMA) is a service used to watch and report on application and system health on a Windows computer.

- <u>Microsoft Nano Server</u>

  Microsoft Nano Server is a lightweight version of the Windows Server operating system that was introduced with Windows Server 2016 for use as an OS layer for virtualized container instances.

- <u>Microsoft Network Device Enrollment Service (NDES)</u>

  Microsoft Network Device Enrollment Service (NDES) is a security feature in Windows Server 2008 R2 and later Windows Server operating versions. NDES provides and manages certificates used to authenticate traffic and implement secure network communication with devices that might not otherwise possess valid domain credentials.

- <u>Microsoft Network Policy and Access Services (Microsoft NPAS)</u>

  Microsoft Network Policy and Access Services (Microsoft NPAS) is a server role in Windows 2008 and Windows Server 2012 that allows administrators to provide local and remote network access.

- <u>Microsoft Office 365 Admin Center</u>

  The Microsoft Office 365 Admin Center is the web-based portal administrators use to manage user accounts and configuration settings for the Office 365 subscription services, including Exchange Online and SharePoint Online.

- <u>Microsoft Office 365 admin roles</u>

  Microsoft Office 365 admin roles give users authorization to perform certain tasks in the Office 365 admin center. Only the global administrator can assign or modify an admin role, which grants the permissions required to control certain functions in Office 365.

- <u>Microsoft Office 365 Advanced Threat Protection</u>

  Microsoft Office 365 Advanced Threat Protection (ATP) is Microsoft's optional cloud-based service that scans and filters email to protect subscribers from malware in attachments and hyperlinks to malicious websites.

- <u>Microsoft Office SharePoint Server (MOSS)</u>

  Microsoft Office SharePoint Server (MOSS) is the full version of a portal-based platform for collaboratively creating, managing and sharing documents and Web services. MOSS enables users to create "Sharepoint Portals" that include shared workspaces, applications, blogs, wikis and other documents accessible through a Web browser. The free version, Windows SharePoint Server (WSS), usually referred to as simply "Sharepoint," is available as a free download included with every Windows Server license. (Continued...)

- <u>Microsoft Online Services Sign-In Assistant</u>

  The Microsoft Online Services Sign-In Assistant is a software application that provides common sign-on capabilities for a suite of Microsoft online services, such as Office 365.

- <u>Microsoft Outlook</u>

  Microsoft Outlook is the preferred email client used to send and receive emails by accessing Microsoft Exchange Server email.

- <u>Microsoft Outlook on the web (formerly Outlook Web App, OWA)</u>

  Outlook on the web is the browser-based email client for users to access email, calendars, tasks and contacts from Microsoft's on-premises Exchange Server and cloud-based Exchange Online.

- <u>Microsoft Remote Desktop Web Access (Microsoft RD Web Access)</u>

  Microsoft Remote Desktop Web Access (Microsoft RD Web Access) is a feature in Windows Server 2008 R2 and Windows Server 2012 that allows users to access RemoteApp and Desktop Connection through the Start menu or a Web browser.

- _Microsoft Scale-Out File Server_

  Microsoft Scale-Out File Server is an active-active clustered file server feature based on Server Message Block (SMB) 3.0 to provide continuous availability of file shares in Windows Server.

- _Microsoft SCOM (System Center Operations Manager)_

  Microsoft SCOM (System Center Operations Manager) is a set of tools for infrastructure monitoring and application performance management.

- _Microsoft Security Configuration Wizard (SCW)_

  Microsoft Security Configuration Wizard (SCW) is an administrative tool used to change the default security settings on a server and to apply a security policy on multiple servers.

- _Microsoft Software Assurance (SA)_

  Microsoft Software Assurance is a software maintenance program that helps organizations gain access to the latest software versions and releases, without incurring additional licensing costs.

- _Microsoft Storage QoS (Storage Quality of Service)_

  Microsoft Storage QoS (Storage Quality of Service) is a feature for monitoring and managing the performance of storage resources allocated to individual virtual machines (VMs) running on Hyper-V and scale-out file servers or cluster shared volumes.

- _Microsoft Storage Replica_

  Microsoft Storage Replica is a feature in Windows Server 2016 that provides synchronous block-level, volume-based replication for high availability and disaster recovery needs.

- _Microsoft Storage Spaces Direct_

  Microsoft Storage Spaces Direct is a feature in Windows Server 2016 that uses local server storage to build highly available and scalable software-defined storage systems for Hyper-V virtual machines.

- <u>Microsoft System Center</u>

  Microsoft System Center is a suite of software products designed to simplify the deployment, configuration and management of IT infrastructure and virtualized software-defined data centers.

- <u>Microsoft System Center 2012</u>

  Microsoft System Center 2012 is a bundled suite of systems management products that offers tools to monitor and automate virtualized environments, including private clouds based on Microsoft Hyper-V.

- <u>Microsoft System Center Configuration Manager (SCCM)</u>
  Microsoft System Center Configuration Manager (SCCM) is a Windows product that enables the management, deployment and security of devices and applications across an enterprise.